Arizona

FOURTH EDITION

by Scott Barker

Revised by
Jill Bean Florio

Guilford, Connecticut

Text design by Laura Augustine
Maps created by Equator Graphics © The Globe Pequot Press
Illustrations by Carole Drong

Library of Congress Cataloging-in-Publication Data is available.

ISSN 1540-1197
ISBN 0-7627-2429-3

Manufactured in the United States of America
Fourth Edition/Third Printing

Contents

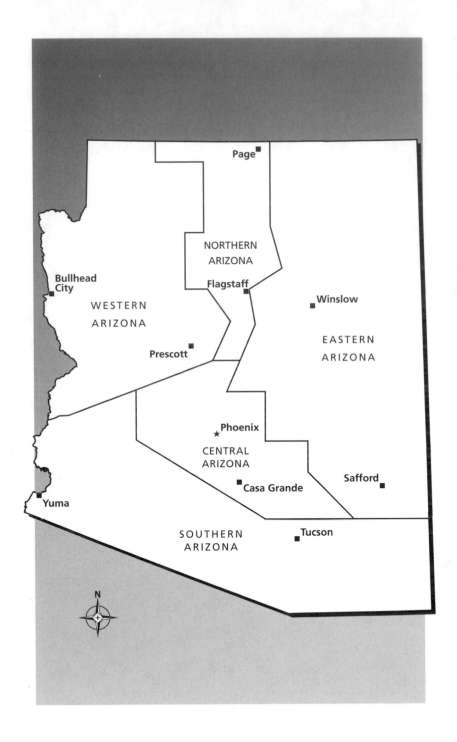

Page

NORTHERN
ARIZONA

Bullhead
City

Flagstaff

Winslow

WESTERN
ARIZONA

EASTERN
ARIZONA

Prescott

Phoenix

CENTRAL
ARIZONA

Safford

Casa Grande

Yuma

SOUTHERN
ARIZONA

Tucson

N

Introduction

Arizona is perhaps best known as the home of one of the world's most gorgeous gorges, the Grand Canyon. It has also gained a well-deserved reputation as a prime winter playground for snowbirds seeking sunshine and pampering. Indeed, it is all that—plus so much more.

Veer off the interstate highways or the main drags of Arizona's diverse communities, and you'll find hidden treasures that the Sunday travel sections often overlook. From secluded inlets on massive Lake Powell and stunning swimming holes in little-traveled regions of the Grand Canyon to an annual jousting fest in the desert and a folklore preserve tucked into a wildlife-rich canyon, Arizona holds more curiosities than any weeklong vacation itinerary could even begin to include (there's even skiing!).

Far from a cultural desert, Arizona has just about any arts-related diversion visitors might wish to enjoy, including Broadway-style shows; resident symphony, ballet, and theatrical companies; and venues for rock concerts and jazz jams. Add to this a generous supply of top-notch museums—showcasing Native American heritage, contemporary fine art, lifestyles of long-gone civilizations, and the flora and fauna of the enigmatic Sonoran Desert—and you'll quickly discover that there is infinitely more here than is often believed.

Sports fans will find their nirvana in the nation's sixth largest state, with professional teams wearing the uniforms of nearly every league imaginable—from the NBA's Phoenix Suns and the major league's Arizona Diamondbacks to the NHL's Phoenix Coyotes and the NFL's Arizona Cardinals. Fans can even root for their own home teams during

Elevations and Temperatures

*O*ne of the most surprising facts about Arizona is the variety of climates and landscapes. It's not all desert; it's not all lowland. In fact the terrain ranges from 138 feet above sea level at Yuma to 12,000 feet and alpine terrain atop the San Francisco peaks. Even Phoenix is at a higher elevation than you might imagine at 1,117 feet. The ride through the center of the state is a nice surprise as it climbs to 7,000 feet at Flagstaff where the great plateau of the Grand Canyon and the Navajo-Hopi Reservations begins. On a recent day in early March, high temperatures in the state ranged from a low of forty-seven degrees fahrenheit in Flagstaff to a high of seventy-seven degrees in Yuma (with Phoenix at seventy-one degrees).

Arizona Climate at a Glance

(Average daily high/low temperatures* by month and region)

Month	Deserts	Mountains
January	66/37	50/21
February	69/39	54/24
March	75/42	58/27
April	83/49	67/34
May	92/56	76/40
June	100/65	84/47
July	100/73	89/57
August	98/71	85/55
September	96/66	82/48
October	87/54	72/37
November	75/43	59/27
December	67/38	51/22

* Degrees Fahrenheit

spring-training exhibition games that bring the boys of summer to sites throughout the state every March. Longtime local favorites include the Arizona State University Sun Devils and their rivals to the south, the University of Arizona Wildcats. For an even wilder sport, visitors should check out one of the many rodeos that are staged each year, demonstrating the best skills that area cowboys have to offer!

Let Arizona's hospitable residents pamper you at the day's end. Nowhere will you find your accommodations as diverse or—in many cases—luxurious. City slickers can relive their childhood fantasies at one of the many authentic guest ranches, and those in search of the ultimate in service and style can choose from dozens of top-rated resort hotels that offer activities ranging from their own water parks and European-style spas to horseback riding and championship golf. And if a day on the links is your idea of heaven, Arizona has a course for nearly every day of the year.

Even film buffs will find a fascinating array of locations that include working movie sets to scenic vistas that have served as studio "back lots" for decades. Wander among the landscapes that John Wayne

Greater Phoenix Average Temperatures

Month	Highs		Lows	
	Fahrenheit	Celsius	Fahrenheit	Celsius
January	65.2	18.4	39.4	4.1
February	69.7	20.9	42.5	5.8
March	74.5	23.6	46.7	8.2
April	83.1	28.4	53.0	11.6
May	92.4	33.5	61.5	16.4
June	102.3	39.0	70.6	21.4
July	105.0	40.5	79.5	26.4
August	102.3	39.0	77.5	25.3
September	98.2	36.7	70.9	21.6
October	87.7	30.9	59.1	15.0
November	74.3	23.5	46.9	8.3
December	66.4	19.1	40.2	4.5
Average	85.1	29.5	57.3	14.0

galloped through, or visit the western theme park that was built for the classic film *Arizona*.

Some of the destinations in this book will have you traveling on the main road; some will take you out where the tour buses don't run. The thing about Arizona is, as film hero Buckaroo Banzai used to say, "No matter where you go, there you are."

For Further Information about Arizona:

Arizona Office of Tourism
2702 North Third Street, Suite 4015
Phoenix, AZ 85004
(888) 520–3434
Fax: (602) 240–5475
www.arizonaguide.com

The Four Corners:
Arizona as Part of a Southwest Itinerary

*I*n so many ways Arizona is the heart of the Southwest. It is home to more Indian reservations than any other state in the union, and it is bordered by several major national parks, monuments, and recreation areas. Traveling from New Mexico in the east, you can develop an itinerary that might include several national monuments and national historic parks (El Morro and El Malpais between Albuquerque and Gallup, Gila Cliffs west of Truth or Consequences, White Sands near Las Cruces, or Aztec Ruins and Chaco Culture near Farmington in the northwest corner). In western Colorado you can visit Curacanti National Recreation Area between Montrose and Gunnison, then continue through the western Colorado ski country to Durango and visit Mesa Verde National Park near Four Corners. In southern Utah you'll find the beginning of the extensive chain of national parks, monuments, and recreation areas that stretches from Utah through northern Arizona to southern Nevada and includes Arches, Canyonlands, Capitol Reef, Glen Canyon/Lake Powell, the Grand Canyon, and Lake Mead/Hoover Dam; also in southern Utah are Zion and Bryce Canyon National Parks. In southern Nevada adjacent to Lake Mead is the everpopular, larger-than-life entertainment capital of Las Vegas. Finally, to the west in California is the Mohave Desert and Joshua Tree National Park.

New Mexico
Navajo and Zuni Reservations (both are partly in New Mexico and partly in Arizona)

Bisti Badlands Natural Area

El Morro National Monument

El Malpais National Monument

Gila Cliff Dwellings National Monument

Chaco Culture National Historic Park

Aztec Ruins National Monument

White Sands National Monument

Colorado

Curacanti National Recreation Area

Mesa Verde National Park

Utah

Arches National Park

Canyonlands National Park

Capitol Reef National Park

Natural Bridges National Monument

Glen Canyon National Recreation Area

Nevada

Red Rocks State Park

Valley of Fire State Park

Lake Mead National Recreation Area

California

Joshua Tree National Park

Mojave Desert National Recreation Area

Anza-Borrego Desert State Park

INTRODUCTION

Greater Phoenix Convention and Visitors Bureau

One Arizona Center
400 East Van Buren Street, Suite 600
Phoenix, AZ 85004-2290
(602) 254–6500 or (877) CALL–PHX (toll-free)
Fax: (602) 253–4415
www.arizonaguide.com/phoenix

Web Sites:

Official site of the Arizona Office of Tourism, with links to many cities and attractions:
www.arizonaguide.com

Grand Canyon: www.thecanyon.com

Lake Powell Resorts and Marinas:
www.visitlakepowell.com

Arizona State Parks: www.pr.state.az.us

Arizona Highways magazine:
www.arizonahighways.com

Arizona Game & Fish: www.gf.state.az.us

Arizona Department of Commerce (including individual community profiles on every city and town throughout the state): www.commerce.state.az.us

Southeastern Arizona Bird Observatory: www.sabo.org

Greater Phoenix Convention & Visitors Bureau:
www.arizonaguide.com/phoenix

State of Arizona home page: www.azcentral.com

ARIZONA'S TOP TEN VISITOR ATTRACTIONS

Grand Canyon National Park (4,930,151)

Saguaro National Park (3,424,051)

Glen Canyon National Recreation Area (2,467,199)

Lake Mead National Recreation Area (2,546,104)

America West Arena (2,338,278)

Canyon de Chelly (2,074,232)

Arizona Temple Visitors' Center (2,000,000)

Phoenix South Mountain Park (2,000,000)

London Bridge (2,000,000)

The Phoenix Zoo (1,200,000)

(according to 1999 attendance figures)

Help us Keep This Guide Up to Date

Every effort has been made by the author and editors to make this guide as accurate and useful as possible. However, many things can change after a guide is published_establishments close, phone numbers change, facilities come under new management, etc.

We would love to hear from you concerning your experiences with this guide and how you feel it could be improved and kept up to date. While we may not be able to respond to all comments and suggestions, we'll take them to heart and we'll also make certain to share them with the author. Please send your comments and suggestions to the following address:

The Globe Pequot Press
Reader Response/Editorial Department
P.O Box 480
Guilford, Ct 06437

Or you may e-mail us at

editorial@globe-pequot.com

Thanks for your input, and happy travels!

The prices and rates listed in this guidebook were confirmed at press time. We recommend, however, that you call establishments before traveling to obtain current information.

Fredonia Area

If you'd like to visit a community that is short in the way of tourist amenities but long on history, you might want to make a stop in *Colorado City,* on Highway 389 immediately south of the Utah state line. The town, called Short Creek until 1958, has been around since the 1860s, when it was a Mormon settlement. When the Church of Jesus Christ of Latter Day Saints outlawed polygamy in 1890, church members who decided they'd rather fight than switch headed for Short Creek. This tiny agro-community became known to church officials and Arizona law enforcement officers as a haven for polygamists, and Mormons continue to be thus characterized by Hollywood and other less-informed folk.

Over the next forty to fifty years, there were several arrests for polygamy, and some questionable detective work was done by agents investigating the populace by posing as filmmakers. On July 26, 1953, the town's male population was rounded up and taken to the schoolhouse (which still stands today), where they were arrested, and the children were led away in the custody of the state. The families were eventually reunited—even in a conservative state like Arizona, the meat-hook approach to law enforcement didn't go over well. The governor responsible for the raid (conservative Republican Howard Pyle) was defeated for reelection, partly because of public disapproval of his methods in this case.

From all appearances polygamy (which court rulings have declared is legal as a religious doctrine) is still practiced in Colorado City. For decades following the raid, outsiders were not especially welcome in town, and one can hardly blame residents. Though the gingham gowns, spit curls, and many other trappings of a simpler time still abound, the community is changing enough to make a genuine effort to accommodate travelers. Visitors report that people here are friendly and more than willing to give you directions or chat about what there is to see and do in the area.

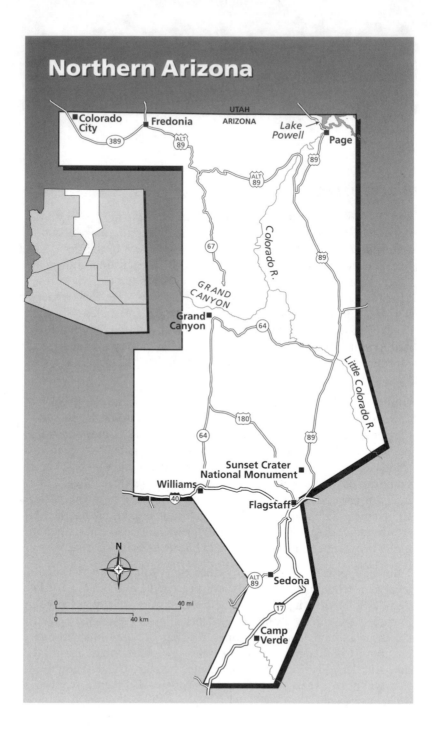

AUTHOR'S TOP PICKS

Grand Canyon Railway

El Tovar Lodge

Lake Powell

Glen Canyon Dam

Black Bart's Steakhouse and Musical Review

Tlaquepaque Arts & Crafts Village

Pink Jeep Tours

Papillon Grand Canyon Helicopters

One thing you may want to do if you visit Colorado City is to stop and watch the ongoing excavation of an Anasazi Indian dwelling in the center of town. So far several rooms, storage spaces, and burial sites have been uncovered, and archaeologists believe there may be as many as two or three civilizations built on top of one another here. Locals also like to go hiking, as there are many wild areas to the north just across the Utah border. The vegetation here is typical of the high desert—junipers, sagebrush, some piñon pines—and there are distinct seasonal changes in temperature: High double- to triple-digit readings are common in the summer, and during the winter the community experiences three or four good snowfalls.

If you get hungry while visiting Colorado City, the **Vermillion Cliffs Candy Shop & Deli** (928–875–8093) at Arizona Avenue and Richard Street is open from 5:00 A.M. to 3:00 P.M. and has a full breakfast menu, along with every type of sandwich imaginable. They also make their own candy—including toffee, caramels, chocolate-covered peanuts, and date balls—and bake coffee cake, brownies, pies, and other goodies on the premises. Currently there are no motels in Colorado City; the nearest lodging is either in Hurricane, Utah, or Fredonia, Arizona.

One of the most spectacular nearby sights is **Toroweap Point** (spelled Tuweep on some maps), about 50 miles from Colorado City off Highway 389 down a lengthy stretch of graded (unpaved) road. The point, enclosed by a guardrail, juts out over the Colorado River, which lies about 3,000 feet below. Because it's closer to the river than many areas of the Grand Canyon are, you get both a spectacular view and a real sense of the power of the Colorado. A lot of visitors either don't know about Toroweap Point or decide that they'd rather see the Colorado from the South Rim of the Grand Canyon, so chances are you can spend as long as you like at Toroweap and not get elbowed aside by other visitors.

A hop and skip east is **Pipe Springs National Monument** (928–643–7105) on Highway 389, where an original Mormon fort (constructed of brick and wood) sits surrounded by high-desert vegetation and trees fed by underground springs. The name Pipe Springs comes from a locally famous feat of marksmanship executed by settler William Hamblin, who shot the bottom off a tobacco pipe. During the summer months there are costumed re-creations of pioneer life, but year-round you can feed the ducks in the duck pond and enjoy the serenity of the remote area. East off

Top Annual Events in Northern Arizona

February

Flagstaff: Winterfest. Sled dog races, llama games, winter sports, snow sculpture, parade, concerts, theater, art shows, historic tours, workshops, and winter star gazing (800–842–7293 or 928–774–4505).

Flagstaff: Snowball Slide (800–842–7793).

March

Sedona: Annual International Film Festival. International independent cinema, documentary and animation, panel discussions featuring leading film professionals (928–282–0747 or 800–780–2787).

Flagstaff: Grand Canyon State Winter Games. Arizona Snowbowl, slalom and giant slalom races, all ages, 5K Nordic ski race (928–773–9707).

May

Williams: Annual Rendezvous Days. Parade, black powder shoot, carnival, street dances, crafts, music (928–635–4061).

June

Flagstaff: Annual Route 66 Celebration. Thorpe Park, chili cook-off, commemorates "America's Most Famous Highway," arts and crafts, rides, entertainment with regional and national acts, vintage car show (800–842–7793).

Flagstaff: Annual Pine Country Pro Rodeo. PRCA approved, purse of $50,000 plus, chili cook-off, fashion show, parade, barn dances (800–842–7293).

Sedona: Annual Sedona-Verde Valley Astronomy Festival. Red Rock State Park, lectures, workshops, viewing, giant Astro-Platform (928–634–7332).

July

Flagstaff: Fair of Life Festival of Arts and Crafts Extraordinaire. Wheeler Park, local and regional artisans and crafters, entertainment, classic car displays, chalk art for kids (928–779–1227).

Flagstaff: Hopi Marketplace. Museum of Northern Arizona, Native American artists, demonstrations, tribal dances, children's activities (928–774–5213).

August

Flagstaff: Flagstaff SummerFest. Coconino County Fairgrounds, juried artists from across the country, fine food, live entertainment, hands-on arts and crafts for children (800–842–7793).

September

Flagstaff: Festival of Science. Promotes science awareness and enthusiasm through field trips, exhibits, and lectures (800–842–7293).

Grand Canyon: Chamber Music Festival. Shrine of the Ages Auditorium, musicians from around the country, jazz to classical (928–638–9215 or 800–997–8285).

Sedona: Jazz on the Rocks Benefit Festival. Sedona Cultural Park, internationally known jazz festival (928–282–1985).

Williams: Labor Day PRCA Rodeo (928–635–4061).

October

Page: Air Affaire. *Hot air balloons, Navy Leap Frog Parachute team, Canada's Maple Leafs, fly-ins welcome (520–645–2741 or 520–645–3992).*

Sedona: Sculpture Walk. *Los Abrigados Resort, traditional Native American and western themes to contemporary and abstract in wood and metal, by international artists (928–282–3809).*

Sedona: Fiesta del Tlaquepaque. *Mexican-style celebration; piñatas, mariachi bands, folklorico dance groups, flamenco/classical guitarists (928–282–4838).*

November–January

Sedona: Annual Red Rock Fantasy of Lights. *Holiday lights, themed displays, holiday music, (800–521–3131).*

December

Page: Festival of Lights Boat Parade. *View from Wahweap Lodge and Marina or along the 5-mile Lakeshore Drive (928–645–1004 or 928–645–2741).*

Highway 389 is **Steamboat Mountain,** a natural outcropping of red stone that perfectly resembles its name. Though there are no picnic areas around the rock, weather permitting, it makes a nice 2-mile hike.

The quaint community of **Fredonia** (928–643–7241), also within spitting distance of the Utah border, was founded more than 100 years ago by Mormon settlers. Some folks say the town's name is a combination of "free" and the Spanish word *dona,* meaning "lady." The suggestion is that the pioneer women probably outnumbered the men, who were frequently off scouting the territory or whatever.

Outside Fredonia, there are several lodges near Marble Canyon, including the **Marble Canyon Lodge** (928–355–2225) and the **Cliff Dwellers Lodge** (928–355–2228). The Marble Canyon Lodge is a sixty-room facility that has a restaurant that's open from 6:00 A.M. until 9:00 P.M., a convenience store, a small trading post, a gas station, and a laundromat. The rate for double occupancy is about $60 to $65. The Cliff Dweller is a twenty-room lodge that has a small convenience store, a gas station, a guide service and fly-fishing shop, and a restaurant that's open from morning through the evening hours.

It's really the natural beauty of this area and evidence of ancient Anasazi cultures that draws visitors. Less than a two-hour drive from the city limits are Zion National Park and Bryce Canyon National Park (both in Utah), as well as Lake Powell and the North Rim of Grand Canyon.

Taking Route 89A southeast from Fredonia leads you over the Kaibab Plateau to the **Vermillion Cliffs.** There are several pullouts and one

Official Arizona

State tree: Palo verde

State bird: Cactus wren

State flower: Saguaro cactus blossom

State motto: Didat Deus (God Enriches)

Official state neckwear (yes, there really is one): Bolo tie

Arizona's largest newspaper: The Arizona Republic, Phoenix

Two newspapers in Tucson: The Arizona Daily Star *(morning) and the* Tucson Citizen *(evening)*

scenic overlook so you can stop and take pictures of these bright-red walls of rock. At the base of the cliffs are some easy hiking trails. One difficult and unmaintained trail—known as Sandhill Crack—actually goes up the cliff. Just south of the cliffs is a marked, gravel road that leads to **House Rock Ranch,** a state-managed ranch where buffalo roam free. This road is passable most times of the year in an ordinary vehicle, although it's a bit bumpy in places and has been known to get washed out. Call the North Kaibab Ranger District at (928) 643–7395 for information on road conditions. The ranch, founded in the 1920s as part of a buffalo-raising venture that failed, is now the state-owned home of a couple who manage the remaining buffalo herd of about 100. There are also antelope, deer, and bighorn sheep in the House Rock Valley area, though they can all be rather elusive. The best wildlife-watching advice from locals is to drive south of the ranch on the 26-mile road until you come to the end. Then get out and walk around a bit.

Continuing east on 89A past the Vermillion Cliffs will take you to **Marble Canyon.** The state recently built a new bridge for car traffic over the Colorado River at Marble Canyon while retaining the older Navajo bridge, which is about 200 feet away from the new one, as a pedestrian crossing. This gives you the opportunity to actually walk out and stand hundreds of feet over the river that carved the Grand Canyon.

The Canyon: North Rim

Named a national park by President Woodrow Wilson in 1919, **Grand Canyon** remains the crown jewel of Arizona's tourism offerings. Drawing a whopping 5 million visitors a year, this natural wonder is a jaw-dropper no matter how many times you peer over its edge. Each time of day and each season brings a distinct palette of hues to the canyon, providing its own unique panorama. A word of caution though: The only thing separating the gazers from the gorge is a low stone wall. Unfortunately, it's not at all unusual for a hapless

Grand Canyon Fun Facts

Age: 2 billion years old

Depth: South Rim inner canyon—4,500 feet; North Rim inner canyon—5,700 feet

Width: 10 miles average

Length: 277 miles

Area: 1,904 square miles

Elevation: North Rim—8,200 feet; South Rim—7,000 feet

Visitors: About 5 million per year

tourist to discover the laws of gravity a little too late. Enjoy the view, but respect the potential danger that exists—particularly for the careless.

Though many tourists choose to limit their exploration of the canyon to the views from the South Rim, there is another, very different side to this spectacular locale. The **North Rim** of the canyon is about 1,200 feet higher than the South Rim, and during the winter it gets snowed in (the only access road, Highway 67, is closed every year from mid-October to mid-May). It doesn't have as many amenities as the South Rim has, and it isn't as accessible.

The North Rim is, however, significantly more lush than the South Rim and has spectacular views. Only 10 percent of the total number of visitors to the canyon go to the North Rim, so solitude is easy to seek out. If you want to stay in the park on the North Rim, your only choice is the **Grand Canyon Lodge** (928–638–2631 or 303–29–PARKS; www.amfac.com). Fortunately, it's a nice place to stay, and the lodge building (constructed of native pine logs and limestone slabs) is built right on the edge of the North Rim not far from Bright Angel Point. The view out the windows of the dining room of this 1936 national historic landmark is not to be believed. In addition to the dining room (which serves traditional Western fare such as prime rib, steaks, and seafood, with some vegetarian items thrown in), the lodge also has a lobby area, gift shop, saloon, and snack shop. The National Park Service also uses the building in the evening for multimedia shows about the canyon.

For accommodations the lodge offers log cabins as well as motel rooms in a structure that was built by the Union Pacific Railroad in the 1920s. There is also a campground on the North Rim as well as a gas station and a general store.

Many visitors to the North Rim prefer to just wander the footpaths under the trees and gaze at the awesome marvel of the canyon. For those who prefer a farther trek, the **Phantom Ranch** overnight to the North Rim includes a room in a ranch cabin, home-cooked breakfast, lunch, and dinner, and five and a half hours of mule riding the first day, four and a half hours the second.

Lake Powell, along the northern Arizona–Utah border, has more miles of shoreline than the entire Pacific coast of the United States.

Lake Powell to Sunset Crater

I t may be difficult to imagine Arizona as an aquatic play park (particularly because the state is more famous for its giant cacti and desert sunsets), but the truth is that this state has a plethora of lakes and rivers that are perfect for any activity from floating and meditating to shooting the rapids.

On the border with Utah sits **Lake Powell,** in the **Glen Canyon National Recreation Area.** Lake Powell began to flow into life in 1963 with the closing of the gates on **Glen Canyon Dam** on the Colorado River. Nine years later, 186 river miles had filled about 100 canyons, creating a playground that includes 1,960 miles of shoreline and boating opportunities galore.

From the Arizona side, Lake Powell can be reached by driving on U.S. 89 to Page, near the southern tip of the lake.

The Glen Canyon Dam and the **Carl Hayden Visitors Center** (928–608–6404) are located off U.S. 89 about 2 miles north of Page. These attractions provide travelers with the opportunity to learn some of the area's history (even prehistory—dinosaur footprints, taken from the canyon, are on display), as well as tour the massive dam and witness its energy-producing prowess. The second-highest dam in the United States, Glen Canyon Dam has a maximum power output of 1,320 megawatts, enough power for a city of more than 1 million inhabitants. The power is sold to independent companies that utilize it in southern Arizona, Las Vegas, and as far away as Los Angeles.

Less than 5 miles northwest on U.S. 89 is the **Wahweap Lodge and Marina** (928–645–2433 or 800–528–6154; www.lakepower.com). The marina rents houseboats and other watercraft, and the lodge provides comfortable accommodations for travelers. Its dining room features an eclectic blend of American dishes and occasionally stages live entertainment. The marina is also the location of a December Festival of Lights Parade, in which boat owners attire their craft in holiday splendor and make the trek to Glen Canyon Dam and back.

One of the most popular ways to enjoy the lake is to rent a houseboat and live on the water for a week or a weekend. These floating motel rooms range from 36 to 59 feet and can sleep as many as twelve passengers. Necessities and amenities such as refrigerators, range-ovens, toilets, showers, and gas grills are available to help you have a great vacation. Some of the more deluxe rigs even offer options like TVs and VCRs, swim slides, and multispeaker CD players. Prices range from $721 for three days on a 36-foot boat during the budget season (wintertime) to $3,179 for seven days in the summer season on the spiffy 59-foot Admiral Class boat that sports a top deck with flying bridge controls.

You can rent houseboats at Wahweap and three other marinas that form an elliptical ring around Lake Powell. For reservations and information on Wahweap Lodge and Marina, Hall's Crossing Marina, Bullfrog Resort and Marina, or Hite Marina call *Lake Powell Resorts & Marinas* at 800–528–6154 (www.lakepowell.com). The latter three marinas are located on the Utah side of the border.

If you'd prefer not to do your own piloting, guides from *Wilderness River Adventures* (800–528–6154) can take you from Lake Powell on a 15-mile float trip aboard a large raft. The journey starts at the base of the Glen Canyon Dam and makes a stop where you can get a close-up view of Anasazi petroglyphs; Anasazi (Ah nah–*sah*–zee) is a Navajo word that translates as "ancient ones" and relates to a northern Arizona Indian tribe that vanished centuries ago. The float trip concludes at Lees Ferry, where Mormon pioneers used to cross the Colorado on their way back to Utah to get married. Still standing near the ferry crossing are cabins erected by settlers. There are also picnic areas and rest rooms.

Tripp's Laws of Lake Powell

*B*oating takes on new dimensions at a place like Lake Powell. Those accustomed to a typical lake will find Powell to be the mother of all ponds and a place where it's easier than usual to run out of gas. Believe it or not you can even get lost on this 186-mile-long waterway.

A map and a compass are essential. A can of gasoline for backup isn't a bad idea, either.

These observations are from a very personal, and slightly painful, experience. On the first of a four-day lake vacation, I did all of the above—got lost and ran out of gas.

Getting reoriented took about an hour. Getting fuel required a tow.

From this, we developed Tripp's Laws of Lake Powell: 1) Even if your boat's gas gauge says you have gas, your motor can say otherwise; 2)At a place with a burgeoning international visitorship, the first boat you flag down for a tow will more than likely be piloted by someone whose native tongue is not English; 3) When you approach Dangling Rope Marina, about 40 miles up the lake, slow down, tie up your watercraft, and top off its tank!

Waterskiing at Lake Powell's side canyons

The beauty of the Glen Canyon area is astounding: clear mountain vistas of sand-sculpted and water-worked stones, high-desert vegetation, and sunsets of breathtaking dimensions. Over the years the region's majesty has attracted many film companies. Notable movies filmed here include *Planet of the Apes, Maverick,* and Hong Kong director John Woo's *Broken Arrow.*

One of Glen Canyon's most famous examples of nature's creative power is **Rainbow Bridge,** which the Navajos call *Nonnezoshi*—meaning "rainbow of stone"—and consider sacred. At 290 feet, it's the world's tallest stone arch. Some of the lake excursion packages offered by the marinas include visits to this marvel, which can only be reached on foot or horseback.

South on U.S. 89 you'll cross the Little Colorado River and soon arrive at the **Wupatki National Monument** (928–679–2365; www.nps.gov/wupa) near the San Francisco peaks. The monument, about 40 miles north of Flagstaff, is composed of more than 800 ruins of structures built by the ancient Sinagua Indians, who moved into the area around A.D. 1066. The ruins include a kind of handball court and a warm-air "blow hole" that releases a constant stream from deep underground. Seasonal mini-lectures are offered when visitor numbers are high. During the summer, two-hour ranger-led discovery hikes are scheduled as well. Admission is $3.00 per person, good for seven days at both Wupatki and Sunset Crater National Monuments.

Because of the elevation, the forests around here are lush with ponderosa pine (the largest spread of ponderosa pine in the world, in fact, sprouts in this area), aspen, and brilliantly colored wildflowers.

Just down the road from Wupatki is **Sunset Crater Volcano National Monumen**t (928–526–0502; www.nps.gov/sucr). Sunset Crater, named by Grand Canyon explorer John Wesley Powell for its orange-colored rim, erupted 900 years ago, leaving behind a 1,000-foot-high cone and a bizarre landscape of lava flow and ice caves. If Hollywood hasn't considered (or, perhaps, been permitted) to shoot a sci-fi flick here, it's an opportunity missed. The terrain resembles something you'd expect to see on an alien planet. Several easy-to-follow hiking trails take visitors around the lava flow, and picnic areas are not too far down the road.

Flagstaff Area

Fewer than twenty minutes south of U.S. 89 is the alpine community of *Flagstaff,* set at the base of one of Arizona's most stellar mountain ranges. There are two competing theories on the origin of the town's unusual name. One says that more than 125 years ago, a flagpole made from a pine tree was placed near the site to mark the location of an underground spring so that thirsty travelers could find it. Historians generally agree that it was so named following a flag-raising ceremony marking the nation's centennial. Settlers chose a tall pine, trimmed its branches, and attached a flag to the top.

Regardless of how it got its name, the city of 59,505 is now a top getaway destination. The town is located in Coconino County, the second largest county in the United States. Over the years "Flag" (as it's known to Arizonans) has been a logging and ranching community and once was an important stop on the Atlantic & Pacific Railroad. In Arizona, Flagstaff is famous for three reasons. It is the home of *Northern Arizona University* (NAU; 928–523–9011 or 888–MORE–NAU; www.nau.edu), which is known for its forestry program; the Babbitt family, who moved into the area in the 1880s; and the Lowell Observatory, which is the site of a number of major heavenly findings.

Flagstaff is a city with a lot of charm. Surrounded by gorgeous scenery, including the frequently snow-capped 12,000-foot San Francisco Peaks, it has preserved many of its historic sites and much of its architecture and thus retains a small-town feel. Still, it has modern amenities that make it comfortable and convenient for residents and visitors alike. The main street, Milton Road, is lined with restaurants (both national chains and local mom-and-pop places), motels, hotels, and shopping centers; it also passes right by NAU.

Milton Road winds north through town and comes to an abrupt split where you can take a hard left and continue up Mars Hill to the observatory, veer right onto the former Santa Fe Avenue, now named Route 66 (which becomes U.S. 89, heading back toward Sunset Crater), then make a left onto U.S. 180, which heads toward the *Arizona Historical Society/Pioneer Museum* (928–774–6272; open 9:00 A.M.–5:00 P.M. Monday through Saturday, donation box at the door) and the *Museum of Northern Arizona* (928–774–5211; www.musnaz.org; daily hours 9:00 A.M.–5:00 P.M.; $5.00 adults, $4.00 seniors, $2.00 children ages 7–17;). The historical society, located in the former 1908 Coconino County Hospital, has an impressive collection of photographs from Flagstaff's early days. This collection includes early twentieth-century photos and equipment from the Kolb brothers, who became famous for capturing the splendor of the Grand Canyon. Also located on the grounds are antique farming machines, an early motorized fire engine, and an original 1880s cabin.

The Museum of Northern Arizona was founded in 1928. The exhibits at the museum encompass the biology, geology, anthropology, and fine arts of both northern Arizona and the Four Corners region. The museum has displays ranging from a life-size statue of a Dilophosaurus (a carnivorous dinosaur whose remains are found only in this region), an anthropology exhibit that traces the region's history back 12,000 years, and fine arts made by Zuni, Hopi, and Navajo Indians.

U.S. 180 also takes you up to *Arizona Snowbowl* (928–779–1951; www.arizonasnowbowl. com), a prime skiing spot as well as a location for snowboarding and other cold-weather sports. Additionally, it is the site of the José Cuervo Games of Winter, with events like a cardboard box race. Snowbowl features thirty-one runs (ranging from dinky bunny hills to some that challenge very experienced skiers). Ski rentals and repairs are available, and you can sign up for beginner or intermediate lessons (also a children's ski school, beginning at age four, runs throughout the season). Lift tickets cost $40 for an all day pass (9:00 A.M.–4:00 P.M.) or $32 for an afternoon pass (12:00 P.M.–4:00 P.M.). There are two lodges—Hart Prairie Lodge and Agassiz Lodge—where you can park yourself at the end of a long day of schussing.

The *Lowell Observatory,* located at the top of Mars Hill, was built by astronomer Percival Lowell, a Mars buff who published a book about that planet's canals. It seems silly now, but Lowell erroneously believed there was life on the Angry Red Planet. He was right on the mark, however, when he predicted that a ninth planet—Planet X—would be discovered. In 1930, fourteen years after Lowell's death, astronomy assistant Clyde Tombaugh found the planet, now known as Pluto, while studying photographic plates. Visitors to the observatory can hear the full story at the visitors center (928–774–2096; www.lowell.edu). The observatory is open daily April to October 9:00 A.M.–5:00 P.M., November to March 12:00 P.M.–5:00 P.M., with all evening programs starting at 7:30. Evening programs include nighttime tours and celestial viewing several nights per week. Seasonal "Night Sky" programs are offered Wednesday, Friday, and Saturday evenings. Admission is $4.00 for adults and $2.00 for children 5–17, with separate admission charges for day and evening programs.

Flagstaff hosts a popular **Winterfest,** voted by the American Bus Association as one of the Top 100 Events in North America. Winterfest activities range from wine-tasting events to jazz concerts to sled-dog races. Locations for the events vary, as do costs (some are free, others have a charge). Call the Flagstaff Visitors Center (800–842–7293; www.flagstaffarizona.org) for more information on Winterfest or other annual events.

In the summer Flagstaff's moderate temperature (the average high is 80 degrees) draws many Arizonans who want to escape the heat that builds up in the southeastern and central parts of the state. The surrounding forest area offers premier hiking and camping opportunities. The city even has an urban trails system that allows visitors and residents to access forest areas, canyons, and national monuments. The Flagstaff Visitors Center has specific maps of these trails, which include treks to the summit of Mount Humphrey (the tallest mountain in Arizona) and to many scenic aspen groves and alpine meadows in the Coconino National Forest.

Special summer festivals include the **Native American Marketplace** events and **Hispanic Festival** at the Museum of Northern Arizona and the **Flagstaff SummerFest,** an arts and crafts festival with food and entertainment in August.

All year round Flagstaff offers the opportunity to hang out in great, funky little restaurants. The **Beaver Street Brewery and Whistle Stop Cafe** (928–779–0079) at 11 South Beaver Street, for example, is an actual microbrewery with an eclectic menu that includes everything from salads and sandwiches to wood-fired gourmet pizzas. Killer desserts include a chocolate bread pudding and a huge fruit cobbler.

Famous Arizonans

*P*resent residents

Alec Baldwin/Kim Basinger
(actors)—Tucson

Charles Barkley (basketball star)—
Paradise Valley

Glen Campbell (singer)—Paradise
Valley

Alice Cooper (rock star)—Paradise
Valley

Clive Cussler (best-selling author)—
Paradise Valley

Hugh Downs (news anchor)—
Carefree

Joe Garagiola (baseball Hall of
Famer/broadcaster)—Paradise
Valley

Andy Granatelli (race car driver)—
Paradise Valley

Paul Harvey (radio personality)—
Phoenix

Arie Luyendyk (Indy 500 winner)—
Scottsdale

Irish McCalla (aka Sheena, Queen of
the Jungle)—Prescott

Dorothy McGuire (singer)—Sedona

Ann Miller (actress/dancer)—Sedona

Jim Mitchum (actor, son of Robert)—
Paradise Valley

Stevie Nicks (singer)—Phoenix

Leslie Nielsen (actor)—Paradise
Valley

Donald O'Connor (actor)—Sedona

Robert Shields (mime)—Sedona

Joni Sledge (singer, Sisters Sledge)—
Scottsdale

David Spade (comedian)—Scottsdale

Sean Young (actress)—Sedona

*G*rew up in

Ted Danson (actor)—Flagstaff

Linda Rondstadt (singer)—Tucson

Steven Spielberg (director)—
Scottsdale

Downtown, in the older section of Flagstaff (east of Humphreys and north and south of the visitors center), shops, cafes, music venues, and very interesting old churches (including a gothic cathedral that has gargoyles on its parapets—a most unusual sight in Arizona!) draw visitors year-round. The downtown shops around the new *Heritage Square* sell everything from outdoor gear to books to local arts and crafts. Along old Route 66 is an amazing collection of motels built during the prime years of the "Mother Road." Some look as if they could use a little attention; others are just as shiny as the day they went up.

In the midst of these nostalgic accommodations sits *the Museum Club*, aka the Zoo (928–526–9434), at 3404 East Route 66. A historic honky-tonk owned by Martin and Stacie Zanzucchi, the huge log-cabin building was built in 1931 by taxidermist Dean Eldredge, who used the structure to display his collection of trophy animals, antique firearms, and other bits of Americana. Five years later the museum was purchased by Doc Williams, a saddlemaker who turned the place into a nightclub. Eventually Don Scott, a former member of Bob Wills and the Texas Playboys, bought the club. For years it was the place to play for up-and-coming country talent. Stars like Willie Nelson, Waylon Jennings, and Wanda "Let's Have a Party!" Jackson shook the rafters. More recently performers such as Marty Brown, Clinton Gregory, Asleep at the Wheel, and local Arizona groups (Mogollon and Redneck) have been included in the Tuesday through Sunday performance schedule.

Scott and his wife Thorna used to live in an upstairs apartment at the club, and some claim their spirits still haunt the honky-tonk (Don committed suicide in front of the downstairs fireplace, and Thorna died as a result of a fall down the stairs).

In 1978 the Zanzucchis purchased the Museum Club, which by that time was desperately in need of repairs, and set about the time-consuming and meticulous task of restoring it to its original grandeur. They succeeded so well that the club made *Car and Driver* and *Country America* magazines' lists of the top ten roadhouses in the nation. The Zanzucchis were given the Governor's Award for Historic Preservation; the Museum Club is listed on the National Register of Historic Places.

Visitors to the Museum Club can study the display of historic photos, buy Route 66 and Museum Club memorabilia (everything from a magnet to an embroidered denim jacket), and listen to live entertainment Tuesday through Sunday nights. The club is open seven days a week. As part of Operation Safe Rides, the Museum Club offers free taxis to and from the club.

Numerous motels, ski lodges, and bed-and-breakfast inns provide accommodations in and around Flagstaff. Although just about every moderately priced national chain has a presence in Flagstaff, two properties are standouts. A venerable favorite is **Little America Hotel** (928–779–2741 or 800–865–1399; www.littleamerica.com) at 2515 East Butler, Flagstaff. It offers all the comforts of home, a twenty-four-hour restaurant, a courtesy van, and more in a pine-shaded setting. Newer is **Embassy Suites** (928–774–4333 or 800–362–2779), 706 South Milton Road, Flagstaff. The staff at this hotel is outstanding and the rooms, well, roomy. ***The Dierker House Bed & Breakfast*** (928–774–3249) at 423 West Cherry Avenue in the main part of Flagstaff offers a comfortable, down-home ambience and nonsmoking rooms. Rates are $30 to $40. Also downtown, another great B&B is the *Inn at 410* (800–774–2008) at 410 North Leroux Street, Flagstaff. Close to the visitors center, this 1907 Craftsman-style home has four guest suites and five guest rooms. Most of the suites have fireplaces and some offer Jacuzzi tubs. Locals claim that the 410 is the town's top B&B, a fact that was supported by the *Arizona Republic* in Phoenix, which lauded it as "the best bed-and-breakfast in northern Arizona." Rates range from $135 to $190 per night.

While in Flagstaff, visit the *Riordan Mansion State Historic Park* (928–779–4395) at 1300 Riordan Ranch Road. Tucked away behind the Target store on Milton Road, this massive, multistory log cabin was built in 1904 for Timothy and Michael Riordan, owners of the Arizona Lumber & Timber Company. The building's architect was none other than Charles Whittlesley, designer of the El Tovar Hotel at the South Rim of the Grand Canyon as well as Old Faithful Lodge at Yellowstone. The National Park Service gives guided tours of the mansion. Tours are scheduled every hour on the hour, and there are also self-guided tours of the grounds. Tour prices are $5.00 per person; the last tour is at 4:00 P.M.

Other must-sees in the Flagstaff area include *Walnut Canyon National Monument,* which comprises more than 300 rooms built into limestone cliffs as part of a prehistoric Sinaguan pueblo. The visitors center (928–526–3367) has displays of pottery and artifacts recovered from the area. The monument can be reached by traveling east on I–40 about 7 miles. (Admission is $3.00 per person and is good for seven days.)

Continue on that road another 26 miles to reach *Meteor Crater* (928–289–2362; www.meteorcrater.com; admission is $10.00 for adults, $5.00 for children), where 45,000 years ago a nickel-iron meteor traveling 33,000 miles per hour smashed into the Earth, creating a hole that's 570 feet deep, almost a mile wide, and more than 3 miles in circumference. In the 1890s remnants of the meteor were found around the crater, and metalworkers, who failed to understand the significance of the discovery, melted down some of this material to create tools. At the beginning of the twentieth century, a mining engineer concluded that the crater was the result of a gigantic meteor, currently estimated to have been somewhere between 80 and 100 feet in diameter. For more than twenty-five years the engineer searched in vain for the main mass left from the meteor. Scientists, including Dr. Eugene Shoemaker, the Flagstaff-based astrogeologist who helped discover the Shoemaker-

Levy Comet, now believe that about 80 percent of the meteor vaporized on impact. All plant and animal life within a 100-mile radius of the site was destroyed as nearly a half-billion tons of rock were gouged from the earth and showered the area.

Apollo astronauts trained in this area in preparation for the moon landings, and some skeptics actually believe that the lunar expeditions were faked on this site! In any case, you can see a spaceship landing in this crater in the John Carpenter movie *Starman*.

The crater museum complex includes the **Museum of Astrogeology** and the **Astronauts Hall of Fame**, which features a space capsule. The park grounds honor the crews of *Apollo I* and *Challenger*. There also are guided tours of the rim of the crater.

Apparently meteoric activity has not been limited to this remote location. If you fly over Arizona and study the terrain from south of Flagstaff to about the Casa Grande area and as far east as Winslow, you might notice a curious pattern of concentric rings that vary in size from 4 miles to more than 100 miles in diameter (you can see the same effect on a raised-relief map). Scientists believe these circles are the result of an ancient meteor barrage that actually scarred the earth's crust. In these circular areas are large concentrations of copper, silver, gold, and other minerals that were instrumental in the economic development of Arizona.

Many visitors to Flagstaff make Grand Canyon their next stop. An excellent way to see this natural wonder is to take I–40 west and drive about 30 miles to the town of **Williams** (800–863–0546), which is named for William Sherley "Old Bill" Williams, a famous trapper and Arizona pioneer.

This tiny Main Street locale was the last Route 66 town to be bypassed by the completion of I–40 in 1985, and with its old-fashioned street lamps and century-old brick storefronts, it offers visitors a trip back in time. When visiting, stop by **Mothball Collectibles** (928–635–2757) on the alley behind the Parker House restaurant and Highlander Motel. Enter from Fifth Street. Mothball carries antique and collectible glassware, postcards, toys, paper goods, and books. **Eagles Nest** (928–635–4203) has, according to the owners, a "little bit of everything," including furniture, quilts, toys, and glassware. These shops are open most days during daylight hours.

For a bite to eat, drop by **Rod's Steakhouse** (928–635–2671), a Route 66 (known locally as Bill Williams Avenue) landmark with a steer-shaped sign on the roof. Rod's has steaks, prime rib, and seafood. Traveling a few blocks west on Bill Williams Avenue takes you to *Tiffany's Italian Shop* (928-635-2445), where you can kick back and watch the big-screen TV while you munch on pizza, subs, and other snack staples.

Williams is also the home of the *Grand Canyon Railway* (800-843-8724; www.thetrain.com). Initially built both for passengers and to serve area mines, the railway carried its first passengers to the Grand Canyon in 1901. Over time it transported U.S. presidents as well as other dignitaries and celebrities to see one of the world's most famous attractions.

Unfortunately the train couldn't compete with America's love affair with the automobile, and in 1968 it carried its last passengers. The defunct railroad was purchased in 1989 by Max Biegert, who restored not only the tracks, the engines, and the cars, but also the *Fray Marcos Hotel* (same phone number as the railway), which now serves as the railway's depot as well as a museum and gift shop.

Using historic steam engines and coach cars, the train not only takes passengers through 65 miles of glorious Arizona territory (which is especially spectacular when it's wearing a snowy winter mantle), it also takes them back in time. While the train chugs along, passengers sit in coach cars that are decorated in original early twentieth-century style. The end car, which has an observation platform, actually uses uphol-stered chairs and sofas. Entertainers, including a singing brakeman, dressed in period attire perform traditional and original music about life and love on the frontier. If you take this route to the canyon, be prepared for some excitement—it's not unusual for a "train robbery" to take place, staged by bandits on horseback.

Beverages and snacks are served during the trip, which begins in Williams at 9:30 A.M. (be at the depot between 8:30 and 9:00 A.M.) and arrives at the Grand Canyon's South Rim at 12:15 P.M. Passengers debark at the canyon's historic depot and can tour the area's numerous attractions before the train pulls out at 3:15 P.M. for the trek back to Williams. You will return by 5:45 P.M. Prices start at $68.12 for adults and $27.30 for children.

Besides being an easy and entertaining way to see the canyon, the train helps to cut down on pollution from the nearly 50,000 cars yearly that—without the railroad—would otherwise all be driven to the scenic wonder. The railway donates a portion of the ticket price to the Grand Canyon Trust, a conservation organization.

The approximately three-hour layover at the canyon gives you plenty of time to see El Tovar Hotel, Lookout Studio, Maswik Lodge and Cafeteria,

Trivia

Summertime temperatures on the South Rim range from 50 to 80 degrees Fahrenheit; in the canyon on the Colorado River 5,000 feet below, they can climb higher than 100 degrees Fahrenheit.

Bright Angel Lodge, Hopi House, and the other attractions in the immediate area. If you wish to stay longer—especially if you want to hike or take a mule ride in the canyon—you can book a return at a different date and stay at one of the lodges within the park.

Grand Canyon: South and East Rims

W hen visiting the popular *South Rim,* begin at the new *Canyon View Information Plaza,* where you will find some nicely presented kiosk-type information about the park. From there it's a short walk to Mather Point and your first view of Grand Canyon. Keep in mind that this spot can be a bit more crowded than some other viewpoints. Several improvements are underway at the park, including the construction of the Greenway, a 73-mile network of multi-use trails on the North and South Rims. In several years a mass transit system will help the park make a transition from the dense automobile traffic that makes canyon viewing difficult on holidays and during summer. There will be plenty of parking there and you will be able to choose between riding a bus, walking, or biking to the canyon rim.

A Scenic Jaunt

You can take a scenic horseback trail ride up to the East Rim from Apache Stables at Moqui Lodge in Tusayan (928–638-2891). The two- to four-hour ride takes you through Long Jim Canyon and allows time to gaze out over the rim. One of the best times to make this trek is in the morning when the sun is rising over the canyon and the colors are deep and vibrant.

The canyon is well-known for its *mule trips,* which take riders through zones of vegetation that range from pine forest to scrub desert. These can be arranged from either the North Rim or the South Rim and cover various distances. A multitude of mule trips can be arranged through the Grand Canyon National Park Lodges (303–29-PARKS; www.amfac.com), including full-day, overnight, and two-night journeys. All riders must weigh less than 200 pounds fully dressed (and, yes, they do weigh everyone!), must be at least 4 feet, 7 inches in height, and, for safety's sake, must be able to speak and understand English. These beasts do walk right along the trail's edge, so the faint of heart may want to find another activity. These treks are hugely popular, so reservations should be made as far in advance as possible.

Trivia

Explorer John Wesley Powell was a brave soul, venturing into such dangerous territory as the uncharted Colorado River and exploring untold canyons—yet he only had one arm.

If you're up for an adventure, legend has it that John Doyle Lee, the Mormon pioneer who is famous for Lees Ferry and infamous for his participation in the murder of more than 120 travelers at Mountain Meadows, supposedly found a gold mine somewhere on the North Rim. In the nearly 120 years since Lee's death, numerous searchers have combed the canyon, starting at **Soap Creek** just south of Lees Ferry, and heading west as far as **Vulcans Throne.** If Lee's contemporaries are to be believed, the gold is still out there. *Note:* Mining isn't allowed in Grand Canyon National Park, so if you do stumble across the treasure you'll have to settle for being famous but not rich!

There are so many ways to see the canyon. You can fly over by airplane or helicopter on **Air Grand Canyon** (800–AIR–GRAND; www.air grandcanyon.com), **Air Star Airlines** (800–962–3869; www.airstar. com), or **Papillon Grand Canyon Helicopters** (800–528–2418; www. papillon.com), or you can tour by bus, using **Fred Harvey Transportation Company** (303–29–PARKS).

A good place to stop on the **East Rim** (though out of the range of the horseback trip) is the **Watchtower,** a Mary Colter (who also was the architect for the Hopi House and Bright Angel Lodge on the South Rim) stone reproduction of a Hopi lookout post. Visitors can climb inside, imagine how Native American sentries felt as they manned their posts 300 years ago, and get an excellent view of the canyon. The Watchtower, on the southern side of the East Rim, can easily be reached by car as part of a driving tour.

Some visitors prefer rafting down the Colorado River to clambering around on the cliffs. About a dozen companies are licensed for canyon river trips. Some offer easygoing, half-day float trips that are perfect for any age or level of fitness. Others do the full-out, go-for-the-gusto, *The River Wild*–style three-day to three-week whitewater expeditions. In any case, you have to book your tour at least six months to one year in advance or there's a good chance you won't get a slot. Call the park (928–638–7888) to find out about trips and companies and to call for reservations.

If you decide to visit the Grand Canyon during a month when the North Rim is closed and river or air tours aren't operating, you're still in luck—the South Rim is open year-round. Of the area's structures, **El Tovar** (303–29–PARKS) is the most impressive and recently underwent a $1-

million renovation. This 1905 hotel, named for a Spanish explorer who never personally laid eyes on the canyon, has the elegant ambience of other grand hotels (like the Hotel Del Coronado, just across the bay from San Diego), yet it has an undeniable frontier simplicity and ruggedness

Only one Indian tribe occupies the bottom of the Grand Canyon—the Havasupai tribe.

that might make you remember the Scout lodges of your childhood. The lobby and common areas are open to sightseeing tourists, and the hotel's dining room serves Southwestern cuisine, fresh seafood, and specialty desserts and has fantastic views of the canyon. The restaurant is often booked solid, so reservations are recommended.

If you prefer a quicker meal, the *Bright Angel Fountain* is a brief stroll west of El Tovar and serves up sandwiches, salads, and very tasty, open-face frybread "tacos." It is part of the *Bright Angel Lodge* (303–29–PARKS), which offers roomy accommodations.

When you're ready to walk off your food, check out *Lookout Studio,* which sells everything from fossil specimens (not from the park, which is protected) to books and videos about the area. At the rear of the studio, visitors can step out onto a balcony that offers a great view and a good photo opportunity.

Another popular gift shop is the Hopi House, a National Historic Landmark constructed in 1904 to look like an adobe-block Hopi village. It, too, recently underwent a $1-million renovation. *Verkamp's Curio,* just east of there, also has many gifts and souvenirs, including T-shirts and the like.

If you'd rather hike than shop, take the *Bright Angel Trail.* One of the most popular trails in the canyon, it is easily reached just west of El Tovar. You should consider yourself warned: It's a lot easier hiking down the steep switchbacks than climbing back up! This hike should only be attempted if you're wearing appropriate hiking shoes and carrying enough water and snacks. You might plan on camping out at the bottom. Before attempting the ascent you can also stay at *Phantom Ranch* (303–29–PARKS), a charming facility that welcomes weary hikers with a dining room and a series of cabins also designed by Mary Colter. Some cabins are basic; some are more plush. You need to make reservations well in advance. Additionally if you're intent on camping, you need a permit and a reservation. Write to Back Country Office, P.O. Box 129, Grand Canyon, AZ 86023 for more information. By the way, you can actually post mail from down here—it will be stamped with the postmark "Delivered by Mule from the Bottom of the Canyon."

Travelers who plan ahead may want to consider scheduling one of the excursions offered by *the Grand Canyon Field Institute* (928– 638–2485; www.tograndcanyon.org). Guides from the institute take small groups of people on hiking, backpacking, and rafting trips throughout the park. Among the unique jaunts and workshops are "Landscape Painting," "Orienteering: Find Your Way with Map and Compass," and "Backcountry Medicine." Special courses are planned for people interested in geology, human history, ecosystems, wilderness skills (including classes just for women), and photography. Fees and lengths of classes vary, as does the difficulty level of the hikes.

Reservations for all in-park Grand Canyon accommodations—also including Kachina Lodge, Thunderbird Lodge, Maswik Lodge, Yavapai Lodge, Moqui Lodge, and Trailer Village—are available by calling (303) 29–PARKS. A full complement of motels can also be found just outside the park entrance in the village of Tusayan.

Sedona Area and South

One of Arizona's most pleasurable drives for nearly all the senses is the route from the Grand Canyon along Highway 180 to the switchbacks of 89A as it winds its way into *Oak Creek Canyon* and Sedona beyond. Especially popular in the fall, when the desert denizens travel north to view the colorful oak and sycamore leaves, the 16-mile gorge is peppered with streams and waterfalls. More than 130 species of birds call the region home, and campgrounds and hiking trails are

Western Hospitality

I can't say I discovered **Garland's Oak Creek Lodge.** *Arizonans had done that themselves. But I'm fairly sure I'm among the first Easterners to know its charms. It was 1980 when Sedona still was a quiet crossroads community with only a couple of resorts, a few shops, and no traffic. Oak Creek Canyon had only its rippling creek and the tow-*

ering red rocks that overshadow it. Somewhere there along State Route 89A I drove over a small bridge and entered a quiet enclave under the hardwood trees. It was love at first sight. Garland's was quiet, peaceful, and simple in a way that provided plenty of restful Western hospitality and yet just enough modern convenience.

abundant. Along the way, numerous resorts and cabins are hidden along the banks of the creek, serving up an interesting array of accommodation choices. *Garland's Oak Creek Lodge* (928–282–3343; open summer only) is perhaps the best known and is so popular with its regulars that many have a standing reservation each year. But others are considerably easier to book.

The Canyon Wren, Cabins for Two (928–282–6900 or 800–437–9736), at 6425 North Highway 89A, is a cluster of four cabins located 6 miles from Sedona and is on the hilly side of the highway away from the creek. Nonsmoking inside and out, the Canyon Wren also caters to couples seeking a tranquil retreat. Continental breakfast is served daily, and each unit comes complete with a small kitchen.

Oak Creek Terrace Resort, (800–224–2229) at 4548 North Highway 89A, is 5 miles from uptown Sedona and features eight motel-style units and nine unique bungalows of varying layouts in a creekside setting. Nearly every unit is complete with fireplace and in-room whirlpool tub; many offer kitchenettes and outdoor barbecues. On-site Jeep Wrangler rentals are available.

Midway up the canyon is *Slide Rock State Park* (928–282–3034), a newish state-run facility that, like its name implies, boasts a natural water slide created by the waters of Oak Creek as they rush over naturally sculpted stone chutes. The area was once an apple orchard, and efforts are being made to restore the original century-old buildings and continue apple production. An original apple-packing barn remains, as well as a 1926 homestead that now serves as a ranger station. For visitors, shaded picnic areas are available, and snacks and supplies can be purchased inside Slide Rock Market. Admission is $5.00 per vehicle.

On the other side of Sedona, another state park is undoubtedly more recognizable—even for folks who have never been to Arizona. *Red Rock State Park* (928–282–6907) has, for years, served as the backdrop for countless TV programs, movies, and commercials. This park is just west of Sedona off Highway 89A and features hiking trails that range from simple to strenuous. Maps of the 286-acre park are available from the visitors center. Admission fee is $5.00 per vehicle. Arizona's state park Web site is www.pr.state.az.us.

If you continue south on Route 89A, in about 5 miles you'll reach the red-rock-ringed community of *Sedona.* Named in 1902 for Sedona Schnebly, the wife of founder T. C. Schnebly, this small town is best known as an arts community, a vacation getaway spot, and a haven for people seeking a different spiritual path. A few years ago Sedona acquired the reputation of being a New Age center. Allegedly several electromagnetic energy sources (known as vortexes) were found in the area, and a wide variety of psychics and spiritual healers decided to tap into them by making the town their home. One New Age directory lists Sedona organizations like Center for the New Age, Crystal Sanctuary, Eye of the Vortex, Global Light Group, and the Third Eye Center. Four areas have been identified as possessing unusual electromagnetic forces. They are *Cathedral Rock* (off 89A and Upper Red Rock Loop Road); *Bell Rock* (north of the Village of Oak Creek, off Route 179); *Airport Mesa* (circling the municipal airport); and *Boynton Canyon Vortex* (Boynton Pass Road, west of Sedona off 89A and Dry Creek Road). Some believe these outcroppings of red rock (the first two named after their respective shapes, and the latter two named for their locations) emit a palpable energy. Each area is lovely to look at, but quiet, serene Cathedral Rock west of central Sedona near Oak Creek is a personal favorite.

Hollywood filmmakers and music video, television, and television commercial producers have long been lured to Sedona, starting in the 1930s when the Zane Grey feature *Call of the Canyon* was lensed here. The pilgrimage continues today with films like De Niro's *Midnight Run* and the Johnny Depp western *Dead Man*. Glancing around at the intense, vibrant red rocks and the lush vegetation, it's easy to see why so many artists also have been drawn to this setting. Although the *Cowboy Artists of America* was founded here thirty years ago, artists of every description in addition to Southwestern have worked here. One of the most famous is painter/sculptor Max Ernst, whose surrealistic works helped to redefine art in the 1950s. Current area artists include Leslie B. De Mille, "shirt-tail cousin" to the famous film director, as well as a very talented portrait artist and sculptor who has done a lot of work for professional golfers. If you're looking for something really unusual and hauntingly beautiful, check out the unique creations of Greg Rich, who uses Gibson guitars as his medium. You can see his work at the *Agnisiuh* (pronounced *Ag-knee-see-uh*) *El Mundo Gallery* (928–282–5622) in Sedona.

Many artists have their works on display at *Tlaquepaque Arts and Crafts Village* (928–282–4838). Pronounced *T-lockey-pockey*, the center's name is a Native American word meaning "the best of everything." Designed to resemble an actual Mexican village near Guadalajara, the center's shops and galleries surround a courtyard. Each September *Fiesta del Tlaquepaque* is held, and strolling mariachis play while children swing at a piñata and food vendors fill the courtyard with the aroma of Southwest-

Tlaquepaque Arts and Crafts Village

ern cooking. Tlaquepaque is also the setting for an annual *Festival of Lights,* an evening event usually held on the second Saturday before Christmas. Luminarias (more than 6,000) are placed all around the balconies, walkways, and on the fountain, bathing the village in a golden glow. The luminaries are lighted at dusk but the festival is open 1:30–7:30 P.M.

Held next door to Tlaquepaque at *Los Abrigados* ("the shelter") *Resort and Spa* (928–282–1777 or 800–521–3131), a first-class facility set on twenty acres, the annual *Red Rock Fantasy* (November 21 to January 11) is a big crowd pleaser. The resort, tucked back off the main road with gorgeous views of the surrounding hills, is decorated with more than 1 million Christmas lights that are lit from 5:00–10:00 P.M. each night. Displays ranging from salutes to the Phoenix Suns to scenes from Babes in Toyland are placed all around. Visitors pay a nominal admission fee (which is donated to a charity) to tour the displays. The all-suite resort has a health club with workout machines and classes, a tennis court, an outdoor pool and Jacuzzi, and three restaurants. *Steaks & Sticks* (928–204– 7849) is a restaurant/ nightclub that combines elements of an eatery with the essentials of a gentleman's club (cognac, cigars, and a big fireplace).

Besides the previously mentioned spots near Oak Creek, there's lots to do in the great outdoors in Sedona. Southwest of uptown Sedona on 89A, then north on Dry Creek Road (the route you take to Boynton Canyon, site of one of the vortexes), you can enjoy an easy 2-mile hike to the 40-foot sandstone *Vultee Arch.* The naturally occurring structure is named after a pilot and aircraft designer who crashed near the arch some sixty years ago.

Sedona—Arizona's Cinematic Star

*V*isit Sedona for the first time and you'll likely feel as though you've been there before—and for good reason. Sedona is a star! Here are just a few of the countless productions—vintage and modern—that have used the crimson canyons as their back lot:

Feature Films

The Karate Kid *(Columbia, 1984)*

Midnight Run *(Universal, 1988)*

The Quick and the Dead *(Cates, 1987)*

Riders of the Purple Sage *(Fox, 1931)*

Universal Soldier *(Carolco, 1992)*

Blood on the Moon *(RKO, 1948)*

Call of the Canyon *(Famous Players/ Lasky, 1923)*

Gun Fury *(Columbia, 1953)*

Television

Death Valley Days

Gambler II

Lifestyles of the Rich and Famous

Sesame Street

Commercial products

Coca-cola, Eddie Bauer, Duracell, Frito-Lay, Kodak, Levis, and almost every foreign and domestic automaker!

If you tire of hiking, several companies can give you a lift—literally. **Northern Light Balloon Expeditions** (928–282–2274 or 800–230–6222; www.northernlightsballoon.com) can take you over the Coconino National Forest for a spectacular view from the basket of a hot-air balloon. Or ramble up twisting Schnebly Road—which affords a great view of Sedona—with **Pink Jeep Tours** (928–282–5000 or 800–8–SEDONA; www.pinkjeep.com). By the way, the Schnebly Road scenic drive can be made on your own using a sturdy, high-clearance or all-terrain vehicle.

One Sedona sight you definitely shouldn't miss is the **Chapel of the Holy Cross** (928–282–4069) at 780 Chapel Road. This magnificent Modern Gothic cathedral was built in 1956 high in the red rocks by Marguerite Brunswig Staude, a sculptor, painter, and jewelry designer who had long envisioned building a contemporary monument to God. Staude chose Lloyd Wright, son of Frank Lloyd Wright, to design the structure, but financial constraints precluded them from moving forward with his grandiose design—a 500-foot monument! Originally slated for Budapest, Hungary, the project was put on hold until Staude moved to Sedona in 1950. No services are held here. Rather, the chapel is open to anyone of any creed to come in and light a candle (for which there is a small donation), study the sculptures (some by Staude, others more than

200 years old), browse in the downstairs gift shop, and marvel at the incredible scenery. The chapel is open from 9:00 A.M. to 5:00 P.M.

Besides the wintertime Festival of Lights and Red Rock Fantasy, annual events in Sedona include the **Sedona International Film Festival** (March), **Sedona Arts Festival** and **Sculpture Walk** (October), and **Jazz on the Rocks** (September). Jazz on the Rocks, featuring about a half dozen top regional and national acts playing everything from swing to blues, is especially popular. It's held all day outdoors in a grassy amphitheater with Sedona's towering red rocks as a backdrop. For information about any of these events, contact the Sedona–Oak Creek Chamber of Commerce (928–282–7722 or 800–288–7336; www. visitsedona.com).

It's not hard to find a comfortable place to stay overnight in Sedona: The area is loaded with quaint bed-and-breakfast inns and has several top-notch resorts.

Despite its small size, Sedona also has a healthy assortment of eateries, from eclectic to European. A fun spot is the **Wild Toucan Restaurant and Cantina** (928–284–1604) at 6376 Highway 179. Located next to the golf course in an unimposing little building in the nearby Village of Oak Creek, the Wild Toucan has patio dining, features Mexican food, seafood, and vegetarian fare, and is open for lunch and dinner. A personal favorite for decent Mexican dishes and arguably

Let's Get Metaphysical! Or Maybe Not.

*I*t was a warm spring day, with the sunshine melting the last few clumps of snow at the base of Bell Rock. After having just visited Sedona's enigmatic Center for New Age (and resisting the temptation to have a photographer capture my aura on film), I took off determined to find myself a vortex.

Trudging through the mud to the sandstone base of the giant bell-shaped formation, I wasn't sure what I was looking for, but was confident that I would find this massive electromag-

netic force. It's an easy hike, so after a good forty-five minutes of exploring, I became discouraged—and felt somewhat silly. Giving up, I returned to my car parked along the highway—muddy and curious. Where was that darn vortex? I didn't see a sign or anything. Relating the experience to a local, I was informed that I had just given up my quest too soon. No, there are no directional signs leading vortex seekers to the spot. Put simply, "If you feel the power, you're there." And I thought that was just the wind.

the best red rock views in town is *Oaxaca Restaurant & Cantina* (928-282-4179) in uptown Sedona at 231 North Highway 89A. Sunday brunch at *L'Auberge* (928-282-1667) at 301 L'Auberge Lane is a special treat, with indoor seating in a French provincial setting or seasonally available creekside dining. There, monsieur, reservations are recommended. Locals point travelers to several choice spots around town, including *Pietro's Italian Restaurant* (928-282-2525) at 2445 West Highway 89A, which houses an above-average wine selection.

When you're ready to move on from Sedona (and a word of warning: vortex or not, the town has a very seductive character, so you may be there awhile), you can either continue south on 89A and head to Tuzigoot National Monument, Jerome, and Prescott (all covered in another section), or you can take Highway 179 south to I-17.

The interstate will steer you toward *Montezuma Well* and *Montezuma Castle* (928-567-3322). Admission is $2.00 per person. The well, actually a collapsed limestone cavern 1,750 feet in diameter and fed by underground springs, is a short distance from the main road. Hohokam Indian ruins dot this area. The Hohokam were an ancient Native American tribe that built elaborate communities based upon agriculture. They populated much of the state until around the late fifteenth century, when they seemingly disappeared, a phenomenon that led modern tribes to refer to these ancient ancestors by the name Hohokam, a Native American term often translated as "those who vanished." A few miles south is the "castle," a twenty-room Sinagua cliff dwelling that was built around A.D. 1100. When it was discovered during Arizona's territorial days by white settlers, it was erroneously thought to be the work of the Aztec king.

Just past the intersection of State Highway 260 and I-17 is the town of *Camp Verde* and *Fort Verde State Park* (928-567-3275). Admission is $2.00 per person. Like a number of Arizona communities, Camp Verde is a great example of Old West architecture—and outmoded cultural interface: It sprang up as a military outpost to protect miners, ranchers, and homesteaders against Indian raids. The fort was built in 1865, and it was here in 1873 that General George Crook presided over the surrender of Apache Chief Chalipun and 300 warriors. Crook is well known in American history as a tough and savvy commander who used Apache scouts and adapted old-fashioned military tactics to work in the rugged and hostile terrain of Arizona. He also forged a trail connecting Fort Whipple (near Prescott) with Fort Apache in the Apache-Sitgreaves National Forest, a road that is still referred to as *Crook's Trail.*

Today this 138-mile trail is used primarily by hikers and horseback riders, with the most popular portion being a 25-mile section east of Camp Verde along the Mogollon Rim, a steep cliff that separates the state's northern plateau from the lower desert. The historic buildings of Fort Verde are now a museum. For museum information, call the Camp Verde Chamber of Commerce at (928) 567–9294. For information on Crook's Trail, call the Arizona State Parks at (602) 542–4174.

Arcosanti sits only a few minutes away, just off I–17 near Cordes Junction. Although Arcosanti is visible from the interstate, uninformed motorists may not know what to make of the odd-looking structures perched on the cliffside and simply zip on by unaware of what they've missed. A sort of glorious urban experiment, Arcosanti, established in 1970, is the brainchild of Italian architect Paolo Soleri. Soleri's theories of "arcology" (a meld of architecture and ecology) prompted him to construct a self-sufficient community that would produce crops and create salable products.

The buildings of Arcosanti look like nothing you've ever seen before: round and square shapes combining in asymmetrical forms amidst walls of basalt, splashed with color throughout. The effect is sort of "Frank Lloyd Wright through the Looking Glass" (not surprising, given that Soleri was a Frank Lloyd Wright Fellow). In some ways the community will remind you of the styles and decor of the early seventies—a lava lamp would look right at home here—yet it all seems timeless, like a fairy-tale kingdom.

Visitors to Arcosanti, which is open year-round, can tour the ten-acre facility, browse in the gift shop (which sells everything from Soleri's famous ceramic or bronze abstract bells to posters and T-shirts), take part in crafts and building workshops, and attend concerts at the Colly Soleri Music Center, which is named for the architect's late wife. Richie Havens, whose incomparable voice transformed the original Woodstock music festival, is a frequent guest, though the center is a venue for all types of music, including jazz and blues. Some concerts are preceded by dinner and followed by a light show projected on the canyon wall.

Arcosanti also has a bakery and a cafe. Admission to the gift shop and cafe is free, but an $8.00 donation is requested for the one-hour tour (offered every hour from 10:00 A.M. to 4:00 P.M.). For information, call (928) 632–7135 or go to www.arcosanti.org.

PLACES TO STAY IN NORTHERN ARIZONA

GRAND CANYON
BW Grand Canyon
Squire Inn,
Highway 64, P.O. Box 130,
86023;
(928) 638-2681 or
(800) 622-6966.
Just south of the park's
entrance in Tusayan, this is
the area's only resort hotel,
with 250 deluxe rooms,
heated pool, fitness center,
restaurants, etc.

The Grand Hotel,
P.O. Box 3319,
Grand Canyon, 86023;
(928) 638-3333.
In the Village of Tusayan
near the park entrance.
Similar in style and
appointments to the park
lodges. Offers Western weddings.

LAKE POWELL
Linda's Lake Powell
Condos, P.O. Box 1258,
Page, 86040;
(800) 462-7695.
Studio condos with desert
or lake views. Located near
Wahweap marina.

FLAGSTAFF
Embassy Suites,
706 South Milton Road,
86001;
(928) 774-4333 or
(800) 362-2779.
Spacious rooms with mini-
kitchens and separate bed-
rooms. Breakfast only
(included).

SEDONA
Sedona Super 8 Motel,
2545 West Highway 89A,
86336;
(928) 282-1533 or
(877) 800-4749.
A good reasonably priced
choice on the main road
with a pool.

The Lodge at Sedona,
125 Kallof Place, 86336;
(928) 204-1942.
In West Sedona, this
secluded bed-and-
breakfast, set on $2^1/_2$
wooded acres, was for-
merly a private home and
now has thirteen guest
rooms, each with a distinct
theme—from Renaissance
to Cherokee.

WILLIAMS
Ramada Inn "Canyon
Getaway,"
642 East Bill Williams
Avenue, 86046;
(800) 228-2828.
A good choice for a family
visit. Activities include pool
and spa pool, hayrides, and
nearby deer petting zoo.

PLACES TO EAT IN NORTHERN ARIZONA

FLAGSTAFF
Black Bart's Steakhouse
and Musical Revue,
2760 East Butler Avenue,
86004;
(928) 779-3142.
Slightly corny, but a lot of
fun, this spot features food
servers who double as
singers—all students at
nearby Northern Arizona
University.

Dara Thai,
14 South San Francisco,
86001; (928) 774-0047.
Excellent oasis for Thai fare
in northern Arizona.

Web Sites for Northern Arizona

Arizona Office of Tourism's Web site,
(*www.arizonaguide.com*), *www.flagstaff.az.us*
has links to the following Web sites for Flagstaff and
Sedona: *www.canyoncountry.com/lakepowell;*
www.pagelakepowellchamber.com
www.www.sedonaguide.com

For outdoor recreation:
www.suite101.com/welcome.cfm/14102

Charly's,
23 North Leroux, 86001;
(928) 779–1919.
Reasonably priced pub fare
and dinners in historic
downtown setting—side-
walk tables available sea-
sonably, patio bar upstairs.

Pasto,
19 East Aspen Avenue,
86001;
(928) 779–1937.
Good, homemade Italian
cooking with just about
everything made from
scratch.

SEDONA
Denny's,
1950 West Highway 89A,
86336.
Home of the Grand Slam
breakfast and breakfast
skillets, plus sandwiches,
burgers, and meals.

WesternN Arizona

Lake Mead and Grand Canyon West

When it was created in the 1930s by the construction of *Hoover Dam* (702–294–3523), 110-mile-long Lake Mead was the largest artificial lake in the world. The dam itself was no small achievement either. Built to harness the awesome power of the Colorado River on the mitten tip of the Arizona–Nevada border, the dam is more than 726 feet tall and 1,282 feet long and is linked to a power plant that can generate 1.8 million horsepower. Boy, just imagine if you could tuck that baby under the hood of your car! Besides being an engineering marvel, the dam, with its Art Deco statues, is a work of art and is the highest in the world. Guided tours are available and depart every ten minutes, lasting about thirty-five minutes. Covered parking (a plus in the scorching summertime) is available.

Just about anything you can do in a body of water, you can do on *Lake Mead*. Swimming; fishing for largemouth bass, crappie, sunfish, channel catfish, and so forth; Jet-Skiing; waterskiing; power boating; wind surfing; and scuba diving are popular activities. I've never dived here myself, but friends who have tell me it's amazingly clear for an artificial lake. If you stay in one of the neighboring towns, you can make this stop a day trip— driving up, renting a Jet Ski, and cruising around the lake for a few hours before heading back to town. If you'd like to spend more than a day at Lake Mead, consider renting a houseboat. There are more than 800 miles of shoreline, which include hidden coves and tiny backwater inlets that are perfect for lengthy exploration. There are countless areas where you can go ashore and have a picnic lunch while gazing at the surrounding mountains.

The Lake Mead Visitors Center (702–293–8990; www.nps.gov/lame), as well as facilities for renting equipment or booking steamboat tours, is on the

Trivia

Though Arizona boasts one of the largest per capita boat ownerships in the country, all of Arizona's lakes except one—Stoneman Lake—are man-made. In fact, Lake Mead is the largest man-made lake in the United States.

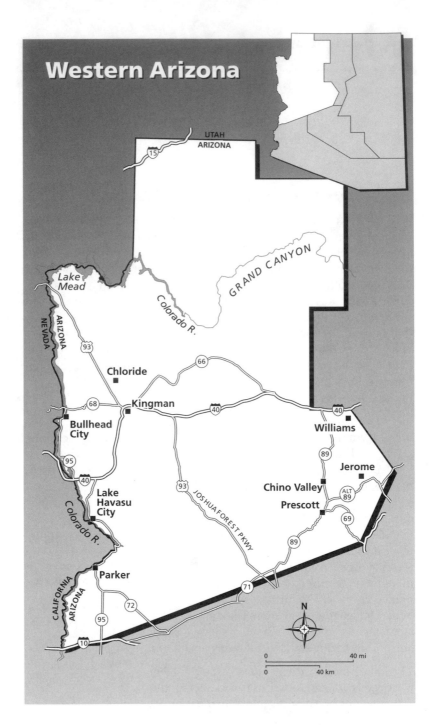

Western Arizona

UTAH
ARIZONA

15

GRAND CANYON

Lake Mead

Colorado R.

ARIZONA
NEVADA

93

Chloride

66

68 Kingman

40

40

Williams

Bullhead City

89

95

Jerome

40

93 JOSHUA FOREST PKWY

Chino Valley

ALT 89

Lake Havasu City

Prescott

69

Colorado R.

89

Parker

72

71

CALIFORNIA
ARIZONA

95

N

10

0   40 mi
0   40 km

WESTERN ARIZONA

Author's Top Picks

Hualapai River Runners

Lake Havasu

London Bridge/English Village

Verde Canyon Railroad

Colorado River Indian Tribes Museum

Jerome

Courthouse Plaza in Prescott

Nevada side. However, the *Temple Bar Marina* off Route 93 in Arizona (928–767–3211; e-mail templebarAZ@yahoo.com) offers camping and boat rental and launching facilities, in addition to a cafe, grocery store, motel, and cabins. RV facilities are also available.

About 40 miles south of Lake Mead on Route 93, *Dolan Springs* (928 767–4473) sits at the foot of the Cerbat Mountains. Not surprisingly, given the proximity of Lake Mead, Lake Mohave, and the southwest rim of the Grand Canyon, this town is a stopping-off point for many recreation seekers. It's also less than two hours from Las Vegas, so you can bet the general store dispenses a lot of aspirin and sympathy! The *General Store* (928–767–3676) at 8424 West Pearce Ferry Road sells everything from live bait to outdoor clothing to arts and crafts made by regional artisans. The store also acts as a visitors center. There is a gas station as well as a few restaurants. *The Jitterbug* (928–767–4372) features everything from Italian to Mexican fare.

A lot of visitors don't realize that just north of Dolan Springs off Pearce Ferry Road on the way to Meadview is the largest stand of *Joshua trees* in the world. Joshua trees are strange, spikey-topped relatives of the agave plant that can reach more than 30 feet in height and outlive most humans. They were allegedly named by Mormon pioneers who believed that the

Joshua trees

TOP ANNUAL EVENTS IN WESTERN ARIZONA

January

Parker: Whiplash Parker 400. *400-mile off-road race through the desert for motorcycles, trucks, cars, rails, ATVs, 20+ classes, (928-669-2174).*

Quartzsite: Hobby, Crafts, and Gem Show. *Displays from around the country, dealers with gems, minerals; jewelry demos (928-927-5600 or 800-969-5464).*

Quartzsite: Prospector's Panorama/Gold Show (928-927-6467).

Yuma: Lettuce Days (928-782-5712).

Bullhead City: PRCA Turquoise Circuit Rodeo (928-754-4121).

March

Parker: Balloon Fest. *Fifty hot-air balloonists with a hare-and-hound race, skydiving (928-669-9265 or 928-669-6464).*

April

Lake Havasu City: International Hava-Salsa Challenge (928-680-0221).

May

Cottonwood: Greater Cottonwood Antique Aeroplane and Auto Show. *Airport—antiques, cycles, street rods, customs, military, kit cars, vintage and experimental aircraft (928-634-7593).*

Jerome: Annual Paseo de Casas. *Homes and historic public buildings from Victorians to renovated miner's shacks; works of Jerome artists and photographs from the Jerome Historical Society Archives (928-634-2900 or 634-5477).*

Kingman: Festival of Arts. *Entertainment, demonstrations, children's art activities, food (928-753-6106).*

Lake Havasu City: Western Outdoor News Lake Havasu Striper Derby. *Two-person teams; $50,000 in prizes; the largest of its kind anywhere in the West (714-546-4370).*

Prescott: George Phippen Memorial Day Western Art Show and Sale. *Courthouse Plaza—juried outdoor western art show, "Quick Draw" and auction (928-778-1385).*

June

Chloride: Old Miners Day. *Vaudeville acts, street dance, gunfights, horseshoe-pitching contest, swap meet, parade, live music (928-565-2204).*

Prescott: Bluegrass Festival. *Courthouse Plaza—top bands, jam sessions, workshops (928-445-2000 or 800-266-7534).*

Prescott: Folk Arts Fair. *Sharlot Hall Museum—traditional arts such as quilting, woodcarving, spinning, weaving, candlemaking; hands-on crafts; music (928-445-3122).*

Prescott: Territorial Days. *Courthouse Plaza—arts and crafts, games for kids, old-time photos, entertainment (928-445-2000 or 800-266-7534).*

July

Prescott: Frontier Days and World's Oldest Rodeo. *Parade, booths on the Courthouse Plaza, fireworks, continuous entertainment, softball tournament, carnival, melodramas, family entertainment (928-445-3103).*

August

Prescott: Arizona Cowboy Poets Gathering. *Sharlot Hall Museum—from all over the West, working cowboys who compose, recite, and sing poetry about their lives and work (928-445-3122).*

September

Cottonwood: Annual Verde River Days. *Dead Horse Ranch State Park—event to develop the awareness of the importance of the Verde River; fishing clinic, sand castle building, rubber duck race (928-634-7593 or 928-634-5283).*

Lake Havasu City: Carrera Regatta. *Nautical Inn—poker run, boat parade, awards for the farthest miles traveled (909-735-7000 or 928-855-2141).*

October

Camp Verde: Fort Verde Days. *Quilt show, BBQ, games, equestrian events, arts and crafts, reenactments (928-567-9294 or 928-567-3275).*

Kingman: Kingman Auto and Airshow. *Kingman Airport and Industrial Park—aerobatics, parachutists, warbirds, Formula air race (928-753-6106).*

Kingman: Andy Devine Days and PRCA Rodeo. *Mohave County Fairgrounds—celebrates local history of Kingman; rodeo dance, parade, bluegrass festival, concert (928-753-6106).*

Lake Havasu City: London Bridge Days. *Free concerts, contests, country-western jamboree, costume contest, parade (800-242-8278 or 928-855-4115).*

Prescott: Folk Music Festival. *Sharlot Hall Museum—old-time fiddlers, folk songs, bluegrass, string bands (928-445-3122).*

November

Lake Havasu City: Festival of Lights. *English Village and London Bridge—more than 1 million lights on display (928-855-0888).*

Yuma: Colorado River Crossing Balloon Festival. *Sunrise balloon liftoffs, sunset balloon glow, and fireworks (928-343-1715, 602-944-4080, or 928-539-2022).*

December

Bullhead City: Christmas Parade of Lights. *Lake Mohave at dusk (928-754-3245).*

Lake Havasu City: Boat Parade of Lights. *Bridgewater Channel (928-855-8857).*

upraised arms resembled Joshua leading the Israelites. Although there aren't any formal parking lots or picnic areas in this forest, you can easily pull off the road and get out and walk around. If you arrive between late March and early April, you may see the trees in bloom. Please note that many maps of the Dolan Springs area show a ghost town called White Hills. As a result of years of pilfering, there is virtually nothing left there, and for that reason, it isn't recommended or even accessible.

Follow Pearce Ferry Road (sometimes erroneously labeled on maps as *Pierce* Ferry Road) north from Dolan Springs to the unpaved Diamond Bar Road, turn right, and in a few minutes you'll arrive at what's commonly referred to locally as **Grand Canyon West.** The canyon's western end is 4,800 feet above the river and very different from its better-known northern, southern, and eastern boundaries. Sprinkled with high-desert vegetation, the canyon itself seems scaled down, more intimate and peaceful. Located on the **Hualapai** (pronounced *wal-a-pai*) **Indian Reservation** (888–255–9550), this wide, open range land has only one blip of a town, called **Peach Springs.** Hualapai Enterprises has recently opened **Hualapai Lodge** (888–255–9550; www.Hualapaitours.com), right on Route 66, that offers sixty large rooms, a gift shop, and a restaurant that's open for breakfast, lunch, and dinner daily. Some 92 miles west of Peach Springs in Grand Canyon West, the Hualapais also offer a 4-mile guided tour to Eagle Point and Guano Point (named after the droppings of the bats that proliferate there). A tour of the rim led by a Hualapai Indian guide includes a barbecue lunch.

Among the lesser-known, although unquestionably idyllic, settings in the area is an exotic canyon located within the tiny **Havasupai Indian Reservation.** Secluded and seemingly untouched by time and technology, the Havasu Canyon appears to be more Hawaiian than mainland, with its cascading turquoise waterfalls and flowering orchids. No doubt

Raft the River

*Y*ou can take a Hualapai Indian–guided rafting trip down the Colorado River. Hualapai River Runners offers one- or two-day expeditions (central reservations, 888–255–9550) starting in Peach Springs, where guides lead adventures down Diamond Creek Road to the Colorado River. This is, incidentally, the only point in the Grand Canyon where you can actually drive to the river. Two-day raft excursions include a campout on the beach. This is not an arduous trip (the guides do most of the work), so it's ideal for adults (and children age eight and older) who aren't especially experienced in backpacking and wilderness survival but want an "up-close-and-personal" view of the Colorado.

the biggest reason for its enduring tranquility is its remoteness—visitors must either hike or mule ride. All visitors, including campers, must make reservations with the tribe (928–448–2237/2141 for camping or 928–448–2111 for the lodge) before entering this little slice of paradise.

Minerals and the Mother Road

I t doesn't take Bill Nye the Science Guy to figure out how the mining town of *Chloride* (928–565–2204), just south of Dolan Springs on Route 93, got its name. Chloride silver ore, gold, and other precious minerals such as turquoise have been found in the area. Much of the area's riches were never mined, and it's not unusual to see modern-day prospectors scrambling around in the foothills of the nearby Cerbat Mountains. Before attempting this yourself, check with the chamber of commerce to get directions and to make sure you won't be stepping on someone else's claim.

If you'd rather look at rocks than dig them, check out Southwestern artist *Roy Purcell's murals.* Created in 1966 on a cliff in the Cerbats, the paintings depict images of a snake, an eagle's talon, the phases of the moon, and a princess, all sort of flowing into one another.

Several sights in Chloride, including the *Old Jail* and the *Chloride Fire Department,* are worth a look. The jail, which may remind you of the drunk tank on the *Andy Griffith Show,* is a two-cell, whitewashed building that's maintained as a museum by the historical society. The fire department houses two classic fire engines: a 1939 Ford Fire Engine and a 1948 Mack Fire Engine, both in mint condition and still in use. On the first and third Saturday of every month, a local group stages shoot-out reenactments and vaudeville entertainment at the new western village called Cyanide Springs. For tickets and information call the Chloride Chamber of Commerce at (928) 565–2204.

The Mine Shaft and Fire Department (928–565–4888) at 4940 East Tennessee Avenue sells groceries and goodies like ice cream and soft drinks. Also available at that location is a public shower, a real plus for campers looking to clean up. The *Tennessee Saloon,* at Tennessee and Second, is still an operating bar located in the former mercantile building that is thought to be about one hundred years old. Next door is the visitors center (800–578–3379) where tourists can get Arizona travel information and make reservations for rooms in several national parks, Laughlin, and other destinations. *The Corner Cafe* (928–565–9608) on

Tennessee Avenue at Second Street serves American cuisine for dinner and spirits, too.

A great way to explore the area west of Flagstaff to the border of Nevada is to follow old *Route 66.* In case you're too young to remember, Route 66 was built about seven decades ago as the nation's first transcontinental highway. Beginning in Chicago and ending 2,448 miles later at the Santa Monica pier, it became known as the "Main Street of America." John Steinbeck immortalized it in 1939 as the "Mother Road" in his classic novel of dustbowl-hardened Okies, *The Grapes of Wrath.* Throughout the 1930s, many an Oklahoma farmer followed the rutted tracks of the Mother Road (which hadn't been completely paved yet) out to what he hoped was a better life in the citrus fields of California.

Traveling a vastly improved Route 66 in 1946, singer/songwriter Bobby Troup wrote a song about this highway—"Get Your Kicks on Route 66"—and different versions (sung by everyone from Depeche Mode to Nat King Cole to the Rolling Stones) were hits in the 1940s, 1950s, and 1960s. The early 1960s TV show *Route 66,* about a couple of young guys cruising the Mother Road in a Corvette, introduced the *American Graffiti* generation to Route 66 and created a romanticism about the diners, drive-in theaters, and motels that lined this two-lane road.

But a death knell was in the air. In 1956 President Eisenhower had signed the Interstate Highway Act, which helped to create safer, multilane superhighways like I–40. The completion in 1985 of I–40 turned much of Route 66 into a memory. Even as the last stretch of I–40 was finished, however, citizens and business owners in the old Route 66 towns of northern Arizona began banding together to save the Mother Road by marketing themselves as historic Route 66 towns to car clubs across the country and lovers of Americana around the world. Today it isn't surprising to drive along Route 66 near Kingman and see a carload of German tourists who've grown up listening to Troup's song or watching dubbed reruns of the TV show pull over to snap pictures of themselves posing in front of Route 66 highway signs.

Driving west from Williams, *Ash Fork* (928–637–0204) will be one of the first places you reach. Ash Fork, named for the area's native trees and the fact that there is a fork in the road going to Prescott, is more than one hundred years old. If you have the time, pull off Route 66 onto First Street (which becomes Double A Ranch Road), follow it across the railroad tracks to Cemetery Road, and turn east. There on a gentle slope you'll find the original *Ash Fork Cemetery,* a collection of splintering wooden crosses and weathered sandstone slabs. The locals say that the first man buried here—Tom Kane—wasn't even a resident. He was a stranger who died as a result of an accidental shooting (so much for frontier hospitality!).

Just north of the cemetery on Forest Road 124, which you can reach by following Double A Ranch Road, you'll come to another big attraction: the *flagstone quarries*. Ash Fork calls itself the "Flagstone Capital of the World," and indeed, these quarries have provided material for countless walls and floors not only all over Arizona, but nationwide via the railroad. The variety of colors and the smooth texture of Arizona flagstone have made it especially popular, and though its appeal peaked in the 1950s, it's still sought after for many types of construction.

Ash Fork also boasts the first *all-steel dam* ever built. This National Historic Engineering landmark was erected in 1898 in Johnson Canyon. The dam is one of two structures near Ash Fork (the other is a stone dam) that were built to create water reservoirs for steam trains. You can reach it (if you have a high-profile, four-wheel-drive vehicle) by taking I-40 east to the County Line Road and turning north. This dirt road bumps along until it reaches a huge cinder pit, where it joins an unmarked access road. Keep driving for about a mile. You should see a large crater that was created during the construction of the dam. You can park here and walk the short distance down to the dam. The mammoth steel plates, which make it look like a massive radiator, are designed to expand and contract with the temperature, and the dam shows few signs of wear after a century of use.

Seligman, just west of Ash Fork, is a sometime stop for Mother Road cruisers (the longest loop of Route 66 left completely intact in Arizona is the 160-mile strip from Seligman to Topock, where this road ends on

Ancient Messages in the Rocks

*P*etroglyphs, left behind by a much earlier civilization, can be seen south of Ash Fork. Head west on I-40 until you reach Crookton Road. Exit heading south, and continue on until you reach Arizona Road. This is a dirt road that shouldn't be traveled during periods of heavy rain. If there's no water on the surface, however, and you drive slowly, you should be able to negotiate it in a conventional vehicle. Continue until you reach the bridge at Partridge Creek. To the right past the bridge, you'll spot a small cliff where the drawings—many of them rectangular symbols, but some clearly representing animals—are scratched into the dark rock. The age of these drawings, along with the identity of the Native American tribe who carved them, is unknown.

the Arizona side of the Colorado River). If you're hungry, tired, or you need to refuel, Seligman has some visitors services, including restaurants, motels, and gas stations.

A better place to make a pit stop is tiny **Truxton,** located over the "hump" of Route 66 where it heads south again after peaking at Peach Springs. Truxton has about 160 permanent residents. A perfect place to stop when you're passing through is the **Frontier Cafe** (928–769–2238) next to the Frontier Motel. The Frontier Cafe, a late 1950s diner that's open for breakfast, lunch, and dinner, serves homemade chili and other staples of American cuisine. Local legend has it that the cafe was originally opened by Alice Wright, who after inheriting a considerable sum of money was advised by a fortune teller to travel 400 miles from Los Angeles, stop at that point, and build a cafe. Today the establishment is run by Mildred Barker, a resident expert on the area. In 1996 Ms. Barker also opened a beer and wine bar called the **Frontier Lounge.**

As for nearby **Valentine,** it used to be that each year many thousands of Americans sent their Valentine's Day cards here to be canceled with the post office's distinctive stamp. A few years back, however, the community's postal carrier was kidnapped and murdered (a terrible crime anywhere but especially shocking here in this small, peaceful community), and the post office was closed.

In any case, the town is named for a former commissioner for Indian Affairs, not for any romantic notions. Film buffs may be interested to know that Valentine's **Hunt Ranch** (off Buck and Doe Road) is featured prominently in a scene in *Easy Rider.* Peter Fonda's character fixes a flat tire in front of the ranch, while in the background a cowboy shoes a horse.

Blink! You just missed it. **Hackberry,** the next stop, is that small. Hackberry, named for a regional native tree, was an 1880s mining community located just off the Santa Fe Railroad tracks. With the development of Route 66, Hackberry had a brief new life as a refueling stop for motorists. When Route 66 was diverted to a straighter path in the early 1930s, Hackberry was left stranded behind the Truxton Wash, and the town dried up faster than a sweat bead in the sun.

Like many frontier towns, **Kingman** (928–753–6106; www.kingman chamber.org), about 25 miles west and south of Hackberry on Route 66, is named after one of its founders. Lewis Kingman was a surveyor whose work helped to establish the Santa Fe Railway. The town is actually much bigger than its Main Street appearance would suggest, with a population of about 36,000. Because it's within a one-hour drive of Lake Mead, Lake Havasu, Lake Mohave, and other recreational areas, it's a major stopping point for camping and boating aficionados.

Kingman is home to the *Historic Route 66 Association of Arizona* (928–753–5001; www.azrt66.com) at 120 West Andy Devine in the restored Powerhouse Visitors Center, which also houses the Tourist Information Center, the Carlos Elmer Memorial Photo Gallery, a gift shop, model railroad store, and a deli/soda fountain. The Powerhouse—which was constructed as a generating station—was begun in 1907 and was fully operational in 1927. By the mid-1960s, all use of the facility ceased and it sat vacant. Demolition was too costly to be considered, and in 1986 the building was placed on the National Register of Historic Places (in all, sixty Kingman buildings enjoy the same distinction). Following a $1-million renovation, the building reopened in the fall of 1997. Organized to help preserve the vanishing way of life of mom-and-pop grocery stores and motels with names like the "Lariat Inn," the association provides some insight to visitors who want to know more about the Mother Road. They also hold a Route 66 Fun Run (where "Get Your

Andy Devine Country

If you're a fan of old-time Western movies, no doubt you're familiar with Kingman's most famous native son, Andy Devine. Born in 1905 in Flagstaff as Jeremiah Schwartz, he grew up in Kingman. He began his film career in the mid-1920s as a Hollywood bit player. His shambling, bearlike gait and raspy voice caused him to be cast as the comic relief in numerous Westerns, including the John Ford classic The Man Who Shot Liberty Valance. Devine also took roles in many vintage TV shows such as Gunsmoke, Bonanza, The Twilight Zone, Flipper, and Love, American Style. He continued working in colorful character roles until shortly before his death in 1977.

Devine is featured prominently in the displays at the **Mohave Museum of**

History and Arts (928–753–3195) at 400 West Beale Street, Kingman. Original movie ads and Devine's costumes are featured. One exhibit looks like the actor's dressing room. Also on display at the museum are artifacts from Mohave and Hualapai Indians, pioneer dresses, World War II airplane nose art (there once was a gunnery school in Kingman), and pieces of turquoise (a lot of which is mined around these parts). For all you Route 66 fans, the gift shop has many souvenirs with the famous road's logo on them. Admission to the museum is $3.00 for adults (children younger than thirteen free), $2.00 for seniors. It's open 9:00 A.M.–8:00 P.M. weekdays, 1:00 P.M.–5:00 P.M. Saturday and Sunday.

Kicks" songwriter Bobby Troup has been featured) every spring, taking riders in every type of vehicle imaginable on a trip back in time with a beauty contest, a car show, street cruising, and other activities.

If you're in the mood for more history, head over to the *Bonelli House,* (928-753-6106) on East Spring Street. This two-story territorial-style mansion is named for the wealthy Swiss family that built it in 1915. Today it has been restored as a museum, and the interior has been decorated with much of the same furniture it held eighty years ago. The home is open Thursday through Monday.

You won't find any bed-and-breakfast inns right in downtown Kingman, but there are a number of motels on the Andy Devine strip, ranging from the thirty-two-unit *Imperial Motel* (928-753-2176) at 1911 East Andy Devine to the 146-unit *Silver Queen Motel* (928-757-4315) at 3285 East Andy Devine. If you're hungry, drop into *Out of the Blue Diner,* (928-757-4433) at 6000 Flightline Drive.

Wandering into *Oatman* (928-768-9448) only a few miles from the Nevada border, a visitor might easily imagine that a time warp exists here—the town looks much the same today as it did when it was established near the turn of the twentieth century. A mining town named after a survivor of an infamous Indian attack, Oatman has braved rough economic times, but its gorgeous Mohave County scenery and Old West ambience continue to draw tourists. Oatman is a big rally point for Route 66 cruisers, including motorcycle clubs, so don't be surprised if you pull into town and glimpse a line of Corvettes or Harleys.

Clark Gable and Carole Lombard, two of the town's most famous visitors, arrived in 1939. After a ceremony in Kingman, they spent their wedding night (though some claim it was night number two) in Room 15 of the *Oatman Hotel* (928-768-4408), a two-story adobe building on Main Street. The hotel, built in 1902, is the largest adobe structure in Mohave County. The rustic hotel, which has many antique fixtures, has a full bar downstairs, a dining room, and a dance floor.

Visitors to Oatman can see staged gunfights on Main Street every weekend, hear live music in the town's four bars, and pet up to a dozen wild burros whenever they wander into town to mooch food. These descendants of pack animals have been damned by some locals as nuisances, but they've also been adopted as mascots.

Another interesting thing to do in Oatman is the *Gold Road Mine Tour* (928-768-1600), which was in production from 1996 to 1998 and produced 40,000 ounces of gold a year. The price of gold seems to determine whether the mine is in full operation, but tours are offered in any case. They take you underground approximately one-eighth of a mile and tours run all day long. Admission is $12.00 for adults, $6.00 for children younger than twelve, and free for children age three and younger. It opens at 10:00 A.M., with the last tour at 4:30 P.M.

Oatman is the last Arizona town on Route 66. A few miles west Route 66 hooks up with Highway 95, which takes you to either the Nevada or California border.

Just east of the Nevada border on Highway 95 is *Bullhead City* (800–987–7457; www.bullheadchamber.com). To reach it continue on Route 66 to Highway 95, then head north. Bullhead City began life fifty years ago as a camp for workers building the Davis Dam on the southern end of Lake Mohave. A rock formation here that resembled a bull's head led to the city's name, but it's now submerged in the lake. The dam was completed in 1953. It regulates water delivery to Mexico and generates electrical power that goes to substations in Arizona, California, and Nevada.

Bullhead City languished for years as a sparsely populated bedroom community. It began to grow in the mid-1960s when entrepreneur Don Laughlin began casino and resort development just across the Colorado River in Laughlin, Nevada, creating a need for visitor services on the Arizona side. Bullhead City was finally incorporated in 1984. Today, more than 2 million people a year visit Laughlin, and many of them launch their vacation from Bullhead City, where there's a $23-million airport that can accommodate planes as big as the Boeing 737. When visiting Bullhead City, stop at *The Colorado River Museum* (928–754–3399) on Highway 95, a half-mile north of the Laughlin Bridge. The museum was opened in 1990. Using photographs and models, the museum has exhibits on local Native American tribes, evidence of European exploration dating back to 1540, steamboats on the Colorado River, and wagon and camel trains that passed through this area. It is open Tuesday through Sunday 10:00A.M.–4:00 P.M.

Lake Mohave can be reached by driving north on Highway 95. The lake has fishing for largemouth and striped bass, catfish, rainbow trout, and bluegill. Fishing licenses are available at the *Lake Mohave Resort and Marina* (800–752–9669; www.sevencrown.com), in addition to tackle and bait. The marina also rents houseboats outfitted with air conditioning, a gas oven/range, freezer, microwave oven, shower and tub, stereo cassette, and other amenities. Smaller boats for skiing or fishing are also for rent. Houseboating is also quite popular on Lake Mead. The marina has several different models from which to choose.

If lounging in a casino sounds like more fun than lounging on a lake, there are eleven casinos only minutes away in Laughlin, most of them lining the western bank of the Colorado.

There are no bed-and-breakfasts inns in Bullhead City, just hotels and motels, although some of these offer valuable options. The *River Queen Resort Motel* (928–754–3214) at 125 Long Avenue actually has an area on the property where you can fish. You can literally catch your own dinner and take it back to your room—or to one of the motel's barbecue grills—to prepare for dinner. The motel also has free shuttle service for guests to Laughlin and to the Bullhead City airport.

For a bite to eat, drop by *Iguana's Mexican River Cantina* (928–763–9109) at 2247 Clearwater Drive. Run for years by a guy locals know simply as "Valdo," Iguana's uses authentic Mexican recipes prepared by chefs from Sonora, Mexico.

Lake Havasu Area

South of Bullhead City and south of the Highway 66 junction with Route 95 is *Lake Havasu City* (800–242–8278; www.golake havasu.com). Founded in 1963, it's one of Arizona's youngest municipalities. The lake itself isn't much older, having been created in 1939 when Parker Dam was built on the California border of the Colorado River. *Lake Havasu* attracts a huge number of visitors, especially in the spring when retirees and college students flock there. In fact, in 1995, the MTV music cable channel used it as their Spring Break broadcast site. It used to clear out in the summer when Lake Havasu City often records the hottest temperature in Arizona—and sometimes in the nation. Today, though, southern Californians and Arizonans alike appear to ignore their thermometers and have turned the area into a popular summer getaway for water sports of all types.

Of course, Lake Havasu City offers more than just fun in the sun. As most of the free world knows, the city is home to the *London Bridge,* all 10,276 granite blocks of which were brought over from England in 1968 by city founder Robert McCulloch of McCulloch Chainsaw fame. When the city of London put the bridge up for

London Bridge

sale because it was too small to handle its traffic demands, McCulloch bought the bridge in a terrific publicity stunt for a mere $2,460,000. What you may not realize is that the city has gone to great lengths to complete the illusion of an English community. At the base of the bridge is the Tudor-style *English Village.* The shops, the streets, and even the phone booths resemble those in London. Tour guides (who are basically there to give directions) and other village dwellers dress in authentic garb. Stores in the village sell curios and gift items—some British, some not—such as glassware and candles.

The English motif continues in enterprises like the *London Bridge Resort,* (800–624–6838) at 1477 Queen's Bay Road, the facade of which mimics a stone castle. The resort has boat docks, several pools, a nine-hole executive golf course, tennis courts, a workout room, and other amenities. Like many other properties around the country, the London Bridge Resort is in the process of converting to a vacation ownership—or time share—resort. When available to the public, they rent for about $99 per night. Many other hotels, inns, and resorts are in Lake Havasu City, but at the time of this writing there were no bed-and-breakfast inns. For the budget-minded traveler who would like to stay close to the action, the *Bridgeview Motel* (928–855–5559) at 101 London Bridge Road provides the services and facilities typical of a traditional economy motel, within strolling distance of the English Village. Rates are $40–$70.

Homesick English travelers (and those who would just like to eat like the Brits) should pop into the **London Arms Pub & Restaurant** (928–855–8782) at 422 English Village. The pub features British ales on tap, and the restaurant serves traditional fare like fish and chips, steak and mushroom pie, and bangers and mash. They also offer American cuisine.

One mile east of the English Village on McCulloch Boulevard, the city continues its re-creation of the United Kingdom. with **Shambles Village** at 2126 McCulloch Boulevard. No, the name doesn't mean that the place is a wreck. It's a reference to old-fashioned English butcher stalls with the meat hung from the rafters. The shops include art galleries and apparel and gift shops. One of the most interesting shops is **Penny Lane** (928–680–9196), a gift and fashion boutique, which features decorative items like handmade picture frames and birdhouses.

Free walking-tour brochures are sponsored by the **Lords and Ladies Club** for visitors who'd like some assistance in discovering the Lake Havasu area. Lords and Ladies Club tour guide John Kany (928–855–7055) takes groups on short trips twice a week.

Another unique way to see the area is on Sea Doo watercraft. **London Bridge Watercraft Tours** (800-SEA-DOO5) at 1519 Queens Bay can take you on a guided tour from the London Bridge up the Colorado River to the **Havasu National Wildlife Refuge.** The marshland here supports a variety of birds, including white pelicans, black-crowned night herons, and kingfishers. It's also possible to see bald eagles in the winter. The Sea Doos (think of them as mini-powerboats) are large enough for two or three people, are easy to operate, and can hit speeds of 40 miles per hour—but hey, let's be careful out there!

The city has a number of major annual events, including Christmas festivities, boat regattas, and the **World Jet-Ski Racing Finals,** held every October. Call the Lake Havasu Tourism Bureau (800–242–8278) for more information about events.

Quartz and Camels

Due south of Lake Havasu on Route 95 is the community of **Parker** (928–669–2174; www.riverinfo.com/parker), and a few miles farther south is **Poston,** a name that doesn't mean much to most Arizonans but that played a major role in one of the saddest chapters in American history. Beginning in the summer of 1942, and continuing until the end of World War II, nearly 18,000 Japanese-Americans were interned at the Poston camp on the **Colorado River Indian Tribes**

Trivia

Palm Canyon, southeast of Quartzsite, is the only place in Arizona where native palm trees grow.

Reservation (928–669–9211). This population made the camp the third largest city in Arizona. Though the detainees were able to create the semblance of a real community by building a pavilion and staging theatrical and musical entertainments, they were clearly prisoners within their own country.

A few years ago, a monument to the camp's detainees was erected in Poston, which still contains the camp's original gym/theater. The monument is a 9-foot-tall concrete Japanese lantern with plaques that tell the story of the internment. The staff at the *Colorado River Indian Tribes Museum* in Parker can answer some questions about the Poston camp. The museum also has displays of artifacts from vanished tribes like the Anasazi and Hohokam, as well as rugs, baskets, and other crafts made by contemporary tribes like the Mohave, Navajo, and Chemehuevi.

Mention *Quartzsite* (which you can reach by driving south on Route 95 from Parker to I–10 and heading east on I–10 for a few miles) to Arizonans, and they'll probably respond "Gemboree!" The fact is that this community of about 2,000, just across the border from Blythe, California, is better known for its yearly gem shows than for anything else. It's no wonder, given that the area is laden with minerals and gems of all varieties. In January and February the Quartzsite population swells to

Quartzite Camels

*B*esides being a rich mining district, Quartzsite once had the distinction of being the Army's test site for integrating camels into its cavalry. The Army had employed Hadji Ali, a Syrian camel driver, to train the troops in the fine points of managing these "ships of the desert." Known as Hi Jolly to his friends, this Middle-Easterner who'd been transplanted to the American Southwest was regarded as a rather colorful character and something of a local hero. Despite Ali's best efforts, the experiment, carried out from the mid-1850s to 1864, was

less than a rousing success. One explanation is that the camels couldn't get along with the Army's pack mules. In any case, the hapless animals were finally turned loose into the sun-baked surroundings, where they met an untimely death as a result of starvation or trigger-happy pioneers.

Ali died in 1902, and thirty-three years later, Governor Benjamin Moeur dedicated the **Hi Jolly Monument**, a stone pyramid topped with a metal silhouette of a camel. The monument is easily reached off the west-end bypass of I–10.

bursting with collectors, dealers, and lookie-loos. Some of the gem selling goes on indoors, but much of the dealing is swap-meet style. Most traders will deal with the general public, but some will sell only to wholesalers. You can find some bargains here, but if you know very little about gems and minerals, caveat emptor applies. Some unscrupulous dealers, for example, will sell polished "turquoise" stones that aren't genuine. Rather, they're made by combining turquoise powder and epoxy resin. For more information on Quartzsite gem shows, call the Quartzsite Chamber of Commerce at (928) 927–5600, or check out their Web site at www.quartzitechamber.com.

Non-Ghost Towns

To explore the west central area of the state, take Highway 89A south and west from Flagstaff. Between Clarkdale and Cottonwood lies *Tuzigoot* (an Apache name meaning "crooked water") *National Monument* (www.NPS.gov/tuzi/). This pueblo, built by the long-vanished Sinagua Indians near the Verde River, is more than 500 years old. The Sinaguans, whose culture included farming as well as hunting and gathering, founded settlements throughout northern and central Arizona, often choosing the land near streams and hot springs as sites for building their elaborate dwellings. Besides the ruins, a nearby visitors center displays Sinaguan artifacts and sells books about the area's history. The visitors center is open daily, 8:00 A.M.–7:00 P.M. in the summer, 8:00 A.M.–5:00 P.M. in the winter.

Named for the tree that flourishes along area creek banks, *Cottonwood* (928–634–7593; chamber.verdevalley.com) has a handful of restored 1870s-style shops that sell everything from arts and crafts to clothing to furniture. There's also an old-time movie theater that still shows (mostly) first-run films. If you have a few minutes to spend, you may want to pull off the road and browse through some of the shops. The real attraction, however, is in *Clarkdale,* a heartbeat away.

Located north of Cottonwood on Highway 260, Clarkdale is home to the *Verde Canyon Railroad* (800–293–7245; www.verdecanyonrr.com). This 40-mile railroad was built in 1911 to take mining and other supplies and copper ore from Clarkdale northwest to the town of Drake. Over time it became popular among those who wanted easy access to the wilderness areas of Verde Canyon. The Verde Canyon Railroad's mining days ended in the 1950s, and after years of struggling financially while hauling coal, it was purchased as an excursion train in 1990. The railway uses renovated New York Metro Line coach cars, each of which can accommodate about 70 passengers. There are also open-air cars where passengers from any part of the train can stand and get a good look at the scenery as the trains ramble through the protected Verde Canyon area, a gorgeous stretch that includes a riparian cottonwood forest, desert areas, and towering red rocks.

The trip also is a wildlife lover's delight. Antelope, javelina, black hawks, and blue herons live here. Though it isn't well known to outsiders yet, more than forty bald eagles are nesting in the area. Peak viewing season is from December through March, when the majestic birds inhabit the canyon, usually nesting within a few hundred feet of the river. During the three-and-a-half hour ride, singer/storytellers dressed in rustic frontier attire keep passengers entertained and help to point out the wildlife.

The railway operates year-round and even has moonlight excursions in the summer. The train operation offers cocktails, hors d'oeuvres, and deli treats.

Clarkdale is also the site of the *Flying Eagle Bed and Breakfast* (928–634–0211) at 2700 Windmill Lane. This B&B offers accommodations in a guest house or in a sunrise room attached to the main house. Flying Eagle has horseshoe and badminton courts and a spa, but the real attraction is the gorgeous view of the valley. The red rocks of Sedona are visible in the background.

Due south on Route 89A, the former mining community of *Jerome* (928–634–2900; www.azjerome.com) is proud to call itself the "largest ghost town in Arizona." The fact is that it isn't a ghost town at all,

Unlucky Day at the First Interstate Bank

*W*hile you're in Clarkdale, stop by the First Interstate Bank. On a June morning in 1928, two Oklahoma desperadoes made the mistake of choosing this bank for a heist. As they began to drive away with $40,000, one of the robbers fired a round in the direction of Jim Roberts, a seventy-year-old town constable who years before had been one of the most dedicated "soldiers" fighting the infamous Pleasant Valley War (a series of bloody range battles between two families of cattlemen and sheepherders) and whom Zane Grey immortalized in To The Last Man. Roberts calmly yanked out his nickel-plated Colt .45 SAA and shot the getaway driver in the head. The surviving holdup man bailed out as the car crashed, emptied his gun without effect at the old lawman, and decided he didn't "feel lucky."

A recent Louis Harris and Associates poll ranked Arizona among the top two states in the country where people would choose to live if they were to move from their current state of residence.

although it nearly suffered the fate of total abandonment. Built on Cleopatra Hill in the early 1880s, the town thrived with the copper industry. At first the land beneath the town was drilled into and blasted out to form a series of tunnels (almost 90 miles in all) from which rich copper ore was extracted. Fires drove the workers out of the tunnels, however, in 1918, and surface mining became the new standard operating procedure.

The dynamiting necessitated by this strip mining caused a shake, rattle, and roll greater than anything Jerry Lee Lewis ever dreamed of, and the town discovered to its horror that it had created a massive slide zone. The *City Jail,* known as the "traveling jail," in fact, has slid 225 feet across the highway since a 1920s dynamite explosion dislodged it from its original foundation.

In the early 1950s, the mines closed altogether, and Jerome languished. But just as hippies discovered the Haight-Ashbury District in San Francisco in the 1960s so too did they find the Victorian buildings of Jerome to their liking, and many settled in the area permanently. Today Jerome is a thriving arts community, with renowned sculptors, painters, jewelers, and musicians plying their trades and professions here. About one-third of the community is directly involved in the arts.

Like many Arizona mining towns, Jerome is easy to navigate on foot, though some of the hills are a bit steep and walking shoes are highly recommended. You may want to explore the restaurants, B&Bs, and shops. Many of them are downtown on Main Street. Shops such as *Aurum Jewel* (928–634–8764) in the Post Office building, *Whiskers* (928–634–7903), a store just for cat lovers, and the *Blue Heron* gift shop all offer unique, handmade items that are fun and inexpensive. (Jerome doesn't attract a huge tourist trade, so shopkeepers have to keep prices reasonable to keep locals coming in.)

Among the historic buildings to see are the *Douglas Mansion,* at the *Jerome State Historic Park* (928–634–5381) on Mine Museum Road, and the Surgeon's House. Built around World War I by James S. "Rawhide Jimmy" Douglas, owner of the Little Daisy Mine, the Douglas Mansion is a rambling adobe home that today serves as the area's museum. The mansion has a half-hour video presentation on the history of Jerome. It's open daily from 8:00 A.M. to 5:00 P.M.

Definitely worth seeing (and staying at) is the *Surgeon's House* (928–639–1452), the restored former residence of the Little Daisy Mine's chief surgeon, Arthur Carlson. Furnished with antiques, the Mediterranean-styled B&B recalls an earlier time when the pace of life was slower and more elegant. The owner has retained the home's charm while adding modern luxuries such as a hot tub. It can be arranged for a professional masseur to attend to your aches and pains. Spiritual consultations and walking tours of the area's highlights are also available.

New to the area is the **Ghost City Inn** (888– 634–4678) on Main Street, an almost one-hundred-year-old B&B that has had many incarnations in its time, including a stint as a speakeasy. This Victorian structure, furnished in original style, has modern amenities like a Jacuzzi. Also worth a stop is the **House of Joy** (928–634–5339), a sometimes antiques and gift shop, sometimes restaurant—and sometimes both together.

Like many small communities, Jerome tends to roll up the streets after sunset, so if you plan on arriving in town at night, make arrangements ahead of time for lodging or food. There are several quaint eateries, including the **Flatiron Cafe** (928–634–2733) at 916 Hull Avenue, which serves breakfast and lunch. For late-night meals, try the **Palace** (also known as the **Haunted Hamburger;** 928–634–0554) for ribs, burgers, and the like; or **Apizza Heaven** (928–639–5554) at 14 Clark Street for Italian fare. Both restaurants are within walking distance of downtown.

A Piece of the Old West

Travel southwest on 89A to the other side of 7,732-foot Mingus Mountain, and you'll arrive at one of Arizona's loveliest towns, affectionately known as "everybody's hometown." But don't call it *Press-cott*. Locals prefer the pronunciation *Press-kit*. ("Just like *biscuit*," they'll tell you). The town was named after historian William H. Prescott and began its life in the 1860s as a mining and ranching community.

In some respects, **Prescott** (800–266–7534) looks like a cross between Flagstaff—because of its high altitude and pine trees—and Bisbee—because of its many Victorian, wood-frame homes. Residents compare it with the sort of communities you come across in the Midwest. Of course, if you're from the Midwest, maybe that's not so exciting. We Arizonans (including Grammy-nominated jazz pianist Liz Story, who calls the town home) think it's pretty cool.

For visitors the town offers bed-and-breakfast inns, hotels, and motels. Prescott also has accommodations that are listed in the Historic Hotels of America registry. The **Hassayampa Inn** (800–322–1927) at 122 East

The pine-forested central Arizona community of Prescott is known as "Arizona's Christmas City."

Prescott was named Arizona's first territorial capital in 1864, a title it relinquished to Tucson in 1867 before regaining it in 1877. The capital was moved—permanently—to Phoenix in 1889.

More than 500 Prescott buildings are listed on the National Register of Historic Places.

Gurley Street was built in the late 1920s as a getaway hotel for wealthy residents of Phoenix. The architecture is Pueblo Art Deco, done in red brick, and includes Arizona's first porte cochere. It has been redecorated on a regular basis without taking away the traditional character of its rooms. Near the Courthouse Square and Whiskey Row is *Hotel Vendome* (888–468–3583; www.vendomehotel.com), which is listed on the National Register of Historic Places. It's a grandmother's cottage sort of place with quilts on the beds and a bed-and-breakfast ambience. Legend has it there's a ghost (and a ghostly cat!) in the house, which may be why the brochure says it's a unique lodging experience, not just a place to sleep.

You won't starve in Prescott: Its ninety or so restaurants range from big-name chains to mom-and-pop establishments. *Murphy's* (928–445–4044) at 201 North Cortez Street is a former general store that is now transformed into an elegant eatery. Murphy's offers three kinds of fresh fish daily, as well as ribs, lobster tail, and other examples of American and continental cuisine. The restaurant's lounge affords a view of *Thumb Butte,* where Virgil Earp—before becoming a U.S. Marshal for Pima County—once ran a sawmill.

If you want to find out more about the area's history, the best place to go is the *Sharlot Hall Museum* (928–445–3122; www.sharlot.org) at 415 West Gurley Street. Hall was an early twentieth-century historian, originally from Kansas, who grew up in and around Prescott. Later in life she purchased the former governor's mansion (Prescott was twice the territorial capital) and began a museum of items relating to Arizona history. On the grounds are the Museum Center, housing the archives and research library; the Sharlot Hall Building, a rock and pine log house; the Fremont House of more sophisticated construction; a Victorian style Bashford House; Fort Misery (which is the oldest log building associated with Arizona); the Transportation Building, exhibiting the vehicle collection; and the Governor's Mansion, built in 1864. In addition there's a ranch house, a schoolhouse, a windmill, and several gardens, including the Pioneer Herb Garden.

Another museum that attracts its share of visitors is the *Phippen Western Art Museum* (928–778–1385) on Highway 89 North. Named after

George Phippen, one of the founders of the Cowboy Artists of America, the museum has permanent and traveling exhibitions. Much of the work presented in the museum involves realistic depictions of cowboy life—roundups, campfires, bronc busting—but there are also impressionistic portraits of ranch hands, Native Americans, and other frontier dwellers that give startling insight into the life, work, and soul of the people of the Southwest. The museum also frequently hosts lecturers and special events related to cowboy art. The museum is open Monday and Wednesday through Saturday 10:00 A.M.–4:00 P.M. and Sunday 1:00–4:00 P.M.

Historic **Whiskey Row** is a stretch of Montezuma Street between Gurley and Goodwin. In the "bad old days" of the West, this avenue of saloons and redlight establishments was the scene of much debauchery and gunplay, not to mention a horrendous fire in 1900. One of the best places to visit on the Row is the **Palace** (928–541–1996; www.historic palace.com) on Montezuma Street in the middle of the block. The original Palace burned down in the 1900 fire, but the original hand-carved mahogany bar was carried (by hand) out into the street and later incorporated into the rebuilt structure. Like many historic watering holes in Arizona, the Palace is now a restaurant and saloon that occasionally has live country-and-western music.

Prescott has been designated as Arizona's official Christmas City, and the town goes all out with decorations and merriment during the holiday season, including decorating the courthouse—smack in the center of town square—with thousands of lights.

There were many Indian wars during Arizona's frontier days, and **Skull Valley,** just west of Prescott via Montezuma Street, which becomes Iron

Chino Valley's Claim to Fame

*A*lthough Prescott claims the privilege of being the first Arizona territorial capital, that honor rightly belongs to the little community of Chino Valley (928–636–2493), 15 miles to the north on Highway 89. In 1863 there was a mining camp in Chino Valley under the command of Lt. Amiel Whipple, and he established the capital at his fort. The most logical choice,

Tucson—a much larger town with more amenities—was ruled out because of its large number of Southern sympathizers. The territorial capital was moved to Prescott the following year. There are some travelers services, including gas and lodging, in the area, but because Chino Valley is primarily a bedroom community, there are no real attractions.

Whiskey Row in Prescott

Springs Road, is named for the grisly aftermath of an 1864 battle between Apaches and Maricopas. The dead warriors were not buried, and white settlers were greeted by the sight of human skulls bleaching in the sun. For years Skull Valley was a stage stop as well as the location of Fort McPherson, established here to protect settlers and overland freighters from Indian attacks. The fort was removed after only a few years of use. A number of historic buildings, however, remain. These include the Santa Fe Depot, which was built in 1898; a one-room schoolhouse built in 1917; a 1916 general store; and a 1925 gas station. Residents like Mary Kukal, who (together with her husband, now deceased) used to run the store, are helping to renovate and restore the old structures. You can see the outside of the old buildings on your own.

PLACES TO STAY IN
WESTERN ARIZONA

JEROME
Jerome Grand Hotel,
200 Hill Street
(P.O. Box H), 86331;
(888) 817–6788.
Thirty rooms/suites in a
1926-era renovated five-
story mountainside hotel.

KINGMAN
Days Inn West,
3023 East Andy Devine
Avenue, 86401;
(928) 753–7500.
A reasonably priced choice
on the main drag.

LAKE HAVASU
Howard Johnson
Lodge/Suites,
335 London Bridge
Road, 86403;
(800) 446–4656.
Orange roofs are the
familiar sign of these lodges.

LAKE HAVASU CITY
Nautical Inn Resort,
1000 McCulloch
Boulevard, 86301;
(800) 892–2141.
One hundred twenty newly
refurbished rooms and
condos, each with a lake
view and balcony or patio.

PRESCOTT
Hassayampa Inn,
122 East Gurley
Street, 86301;
(800) 322–1927.
Sixty-eight rooms and
suites. Peacock Dining

Room and cocktail lounge. Charming ambience and service. Listed in the National Register of Historic Places and rumored to be haunted.

Hotel Vendome, 230 South Cortez Street, 86303; (888) 468-3583. Twenty-one rooms and suites within walking distance of Courthouse Plaza, museums, and shops. Wine and beer bar, cozy lobby. Listed on National Register of Historic Places.

Comfort Inn, 1290 White Spar Road, 86305; (928) 778-5770 or (800) 228-5150. A reasonably priced choice on the continuation of Montezuma Street on Highway 89.

PLACES TO EAT IN WESTERN ARIZONA

COTTONWOOD
Peter Piper Pizza, 2780 East Highway 89A, 86326; (928) 634-8218. Great for a quick, easy meal.

KINGMAN
Cracker Barrel Restaurant, 3520 Stockton Hill Road, 86401. Family restaurant in the Western tradition.

PRESCOTT
Red Lobster, 1821 East Highway 69, 86303; (928) 778-2717. Seafood is the specialty, plus chicken, salads, and soups.

YUMA
Bella Vita, 2755 South Fourth Avenue, 85364; (928) 344-3989. This family-owned Italian spot is known locally for its huge portions and delicious, authentic fare. Don't let its "hole-in-the-wall" location fool you. It's worth a stop for a moderately priced meal. Open daily, 11:00 A.M. to 10:00 P.M.

The Crossing, 2680 South Fourth Avenue, 85364; (928) 726-5551. Talk about selection! From steak and prime rib to burgers, seafood, and pasta, the Crossing has a little something for everyone at prices that won't break the bank. Hours are 11:00 A.M. to 9:30 P.M., Monday to Saturday; 11:00 A.M. to 8:00 P.M. Sunday.

Web Sites for Western Arizona

Arizona Office of Tourism's Web site *www.arizonaguide.com*, has links to Web sites for the following cities:

Hualapi Indian Nation, Kingman, Lake Havasu City, and Yuma.

Eastern Arizona

The Navajo and Hopi Reservations

It's estimated that the *Navajo and Hopi Indian Reservations* cover a staggering 25,000 square miles of northeastern Arizona, southeastern Utah, southwestern Colorado, and northwestern Utah—a region known as the four corners region—making it larger than West Virginia. With a population of less than a quarter million, it's easy to figure out that there are many miles of wide-open territory without a human being in sight. You can see vast expanses of unbroken near-wilderness area, then, suddenly, modern homes or a collection of hogans—traditional, one-room, six-sided Navajo dwellings—pop into view. The solitude of the land is a keen reminder of what this country was like hundreds of years ago.

Therein lies one of the primary attractions of *Navajoland* (928–871–6436/7371; www.navajo.org), along with one of the biggest problems for travelers. Few people means plenty of areas with no automotive services, so if your radiator overheats, you break an axle on a rutted road, or you just get very hungry, you can be out of luck.

Here's some advice for anyone planning a trip to the reservation:

1. Buy a good (detailed, showing dirt roads) map of the area, and plan your route well in advance. This will save a lot of aimless driving.

2. Make sure your vehicle is in tip-top physical shape. Check fan belts, hoses, all fluid levels, tires, and so on. If anything seems suspiciously close to being worn-out or broken, have it fixed. If it's a rental vehicle, trade it in for a new one.

3. Calculate distance and gas mileage. There may not be a service station for many, many miles, so make sure you have more than enough fuel to reach your destination and get back. Whenever you come to a gas station, top off your tank.

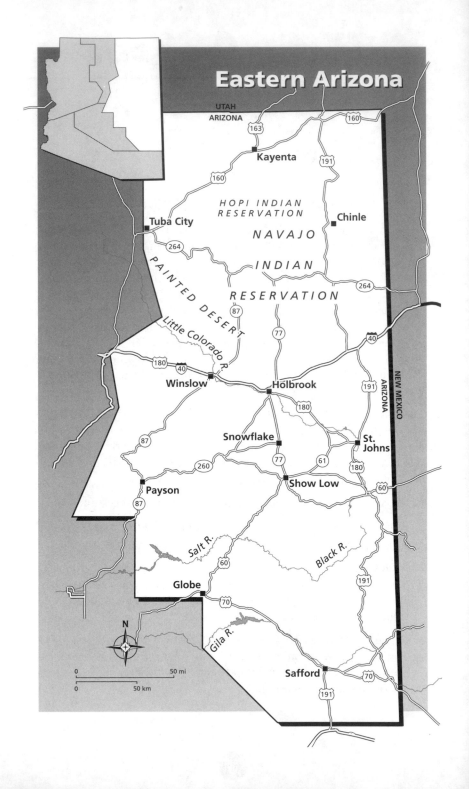

Eastern Arizona

UTAH
ARIZONA

163

160

191

Kayenta

HOPI INDIAN
RESERVATION

Tuba City

Chinle

NAVAJO

264

INDIAN

RESERVATION

264

P A I N T E D   D E S E R T

87

Little Colorado R.

77

40

180

40

Winslow

Holbrook

191

NEW MEXICO
ARIZONA

180

87

Snowflake

St. Johns

260

77

61

180

Payson

87

Show Low

60

Salt R.

Black R.

60

191

Globe

70

N

Gila R.

0   50 mi
0   50 km

Safford

70

191

4. If you want to go somewhere other than the Navajo Reservation visitors center (which is at Window Rock, near the New Mexico border at the junction of I–40 and Indian Route 12), take a vehicle that has adequate ground clearance for rough roads. A truck or four-wheel-drive vehicle is best here. The main roads up to the reservation and to the prime attractions (for example, trading posts) are usually in good shape, but the pathways to Indian ruins and some of the more remote villages are unpaved. These are not all-weather roads, and your $40,000 sporty import—with its touchy race-tuned suspension—will be pounded into an expensive bucket of metric bolts by the time you get where you're going.

5. Travel in good weather. Again, many roads are unpaved and become all but impassable in snow or heavy rain.

6. Bring provisions in a cooler: water, trail mix, and fruit that travels well (like oranges).

And keep this very important fact in mind: When you enter the reservation, you're actually entering another nation's territory. Show respect for its laws, customs, and culture. A good practice is to stop at the visitors center first and get the rundown on what you can and can't do on the reservation. You may not be allowed to attend certain ceremonies, and at others you may be required to dress conservatively (no shorts and Hawaiian shirts). Alcohol is generally outlawed on reservation land.

In general, cameras, camcorders, tape recorders, and sketch pads are forbidden in the villages. Visitors who want some record of the colorful, expressive ceremonies or powwows will have to rely on memory to preserve that experience. Occasionally Native American tribes will stage dance or drum competitions (often off the reservations) where cameras and recorders are allowed.

While you're driving, you'll notice that in many well-traveled areas of the reservation roadside vendors sell everything from katsina dolls (which are made to teach children about Hopi Katsina spirits) to rugs, baskets, pottery, and jewelry. If your interest is only in fine arts, you should be cautious when buying these arts and crafts. An experienced dealer in Native American art advises as follows: "Most good artists are going to show and sell either directly to their own clients or to galleries." Some work you see is of inferior quality or it may actually be Mexican in origin.

TOP ANNUAL EVENTS IN EASTERN ARIZONA

January

Alpine: Sled Dog Races. Arizona Mountain Mushers, ski jouring and sled doffing competition (928–339–4330).

Holbrook: Hashknife Pony Express Ride. From Hollbrook to Scottsdale, swearing-in ceremonies, predinner ride (928–524–6558 or 800–524–2459).

February

Globe/Miami: Historic Home and Antique & Quilt Show. Transportation is provided by tour guides (928–425–4495 or 800–804–5623).

March

Superior: Welcome Back Buzzards. Boyce Thompson Arboretum, local flock of turkey vultures are due back to their roosts in the eucalyptus grove, bird-watching tour follows buzzard viewing (928–689–2811).

April

Miami: Mining Country Boom Town Spree. Old-fashioned mining competitions, a wild bed race through the streets, arts and crafts (928–473–4403 or 473–3673).

Tsaile: Navajo Community College Powwow. (928–724–6741 or 928–724–6743).

June

Strawberry: Strawberry Festival. Community Center, seventy-plus arts and crafts booths, food (928–476–3547 or 800–672–9766).

Hollbrook: Old West Celebration and Painted Desert Classic. Arts and crafts, kid's games, foot races, fun run, Native American song and dance, quilt auction (928–524–6558 or 800–524–2459).

August

Chinle: Central Navajo Fair. All-Indian rodeo, carnival, arts and crafts market, powwow, Miss Central Navajo pageant, western concert, 4-H exhibit (928–674–2052).

Eager: Eager Daze. Concert featuring national entertainer, car show, arts and crafts, kid's zone, logging competition, and bluegrass (928–333–4128).

Payson: World's Oldest Continuous Rodeo. Indian dancers, floats, mountain men (928–474–4515 or 800–672–9766).

September

Overgaard: Oktoberfest in the Pines. German food/beer, arts and crafts, children's games, horseshoe tournament (928–535–4406).

Payson: State Championship Old Time Fiddlers Contest. Cowboy poets, storytellers, country and bluegrass music, children's music workshop, crafts, fiddle makers, leather workers (928–474–3398 or 800–672–9766).

Safford/Thatcher: Gila Valley Cowboy Poetry and Music Gathering (928–428–2511 or 888–837–1841).

Whiteriver: White Mountain Apache Tribal Fair and Rodeo. More than seventy years old, features all-Indian rodeos, concerts, carnival, exhibits, competition (928–338–4346).

Window Rock: Navajo Nation Fair. More than fifty years old, features arts and crafts, contests, exhibits, concerts, horse racing, powwow, rodeo, traditional song and dance (928–871–6703 or 928–871–6478).

Winslow: West's Best Rodeo. Southwest Cowboys Association open rodeo (928–289–4022).

Winslow: Heritage Days. Entertainment, dancers, music, talent show, rodeo, skateboarding competition, carnival, arts and crafts (928–289–5714).

October

Globe/Miami: Apache Jii Day. All Indian celebration, crafts, paintings, baskets, quilts, dolls and clothing, entertainment by various tribes (800–804–5623).

November

Safford: Cowboy Christmas Arts and Crafts Show (928–428–5990).

San Carlos: Veterans' Memorial Fair, Pageant, and Rodeo. Powwow, carnival and all-Indian rodeo (650–475–2361).

Superior: Feeling of Fall Festival. Boyce Thompson Arboretum, the sights and smells of fall, Arizona apple cider, apple pie and doughnuts, live music, special events for kids (928–689–2811).

Winslow: Christmas Parade. More than fifty years old, features Arizona's largest Christmas parade (928–289–2434 or 928–289–2435).

December

Globe/Miami: Festival of Lights. Besh-Ba-Gowah Archaeological Park, luminarias, Christmas program and bonfire (520–425–0320 or 800–804–5623).

Unless you don't mind this, or you simply want a souvenir, stick with well-established galleries and shops. The visitors center will tell you what and where they are and can also direct you to the homes of artists and craftspeople who sell directly to the public.

Native American craftspeople can spend months or even longer working on a single piece. A lot of time and painstaking work have gone into creating the olla (*oy-yah,* a pot), bracelet, or finely woven rug you're handling. The artist has a good idea of how much it's worth. There are definite established prices, and trying to haggle over money is usually considered an insult.

Though Native American art is often cross-cultural (for example, every tribe has its share of oil painters and sculptors), as a rule of thumb the Navajos are best known for weaving and jewelry, Hopis are revered for their katsina dolls, Zunis are respected for their fetishes and jewelry, and Tohono O'odham (pronounced *Tahano Autum*) and Pima Indians are known for basketry.

In recent years, Native American artwork—everything from Pima ollas to Zuni bracelets—has become highly collectible. Blankets and rugs from the 1880s or earlier can sell for hundreds of thousands of dollars. Experts predict that prices for the works of contemporary Native American artists, who often spend as long as a year laboring on a single rug or other piece, will continue to rise. (Recently a woman who had purchased a pot some thirty years ago on a reservation for $50 had it appraised for $5,000.)

Some trading posts are worth a visit if for no other reason than to marvel at their wealth of marvelous arts and crafts as well as their sense of history. One of the best places to look or buy is the **Hubbell Trading Post** (928–755–3475; www.nps.gov/hutr), about a mile west of the tiny town of **Ganado** off Highway 264 west of Window Rock. Founded in 1878 by John Lorenzo Hubbell, this establishment has been frequented by celebrities, visiting dignitaries, and U.S. presidents. If you can't find the katsina doll, basket, or blanket you want here, it probably doesn't exist. Next door to the trading post at the visitors center, you can take a self-guided tour and see exhibits on Hubbell and the history of trading posts on the western frontier. Quite often Native American artisans use the area around the visitors center as a work space, and for a tip of a few dollars they'll pose for pictures.

The best place to start an exploration of the Navajo Reservation is the pueblo-style complex that houses the **Cameron Trading Post, Motel, and Restaurant** (800–338–7385; www.camerontradingpost.com/index. html). This eighty-year-old series of stone and wood structures was recently renovated. The hotel features two-story or three-story rooms decorated in a rustic Southwestern style. The restaurant has specialties like Navajo stew and fry bread, as well as traditional burgers and sandwiches. More spectacular than the food, however, is the view from the dining room of the Little Colorado River. The trading post offers a vast assortment of katsinas, rugs, baskets, sand paintings, and pottery. Additionally, an attached gallery has high-end items, including ceremonial headdresses. Prices in the trading post and gallery are reasonable, and you can be assured of the authenticity.

Motorists unfamiliar with this vast land should understand that though many towns appear on the typical road map, services like food, water, and gasoline can be dozens of miles apart. Heading toward Kayenta and Monument Valley, the town of **Tuba City**, near the intersection of Highways 160 and 264, is a good place to stop, fill up, and stock up on supplies.

Another stop you might want to make on the way to Monument Valley is the **Kayenta Trading Post** (928–697–8611) at 1000 Main Street off Highway 163 in the town of **Kayenta.** The post, which has existed for about forty years, offers everything from Native American jewelry, pottery, and rugs to retail groceries, videotape rentals, and even chicken feed. The store's exterior walls now sport Navajo creation-story murals, painted in 2001 by famed Navajo artist Carlos Begay.

The capital of the Navajo Nation is **Window Rock,** located on Route 264 just a few miles west of the New Mexico border. There are several interesting attractions near Window Rock. About 3 miles west on Highway 264 you'll see the **St. Michaels Historical Museum** (928–871–4171). This stone building was a home for Franciscan friars during the 1890s.

Native American Art

*H*aving once made the mistake of not buying a piece of Indian pottery that by now would have doubled or tripled in value, I've decided it's high time I learned. Now living in Arizona I understand and appreciate so much of what the Indian cultures of our country are all about. For one thing their love of the land is saving the open spaces of the West. Their reverence for the earth is also reflected in their pottery, made from the rich clay of the Arizona mesas. Utilitarian in origin, native pottery is an art form that dates back 2,000 years. Each tribe has its own way of decorating and coloring their grain and water pots—Hopi Tewa pottery is distinguished by the intricacy of their designs; Zuni use an owl motif; and the Acomas prefer figures of both animals and birds. The Navajos are known for their weaving, which is a 300-year-old craft passed from mothers to daughters, possibly with a grandmother also providing both instruction and tribal lore as part of the learning process. There

are more than thirty styles of Navajo rugs, each named for the various regions of their vast reservation (nearly five million acres in total size). Geometric shapes and representations of their deities are the distinguishing features. Katsina dolls are a Hopi tradition given as gifts and teaching tools to their children. Carved from the root of a cottonwood tree, they represent dancers and spiritual beings who carry the prayers of the living to the deities who control events of everyday life. Women are particularly fond of buying native American jewelry when they visit Arizona. The Navajos and the Zunis are the tribes associated with necklaces, bracelets, rings, belts, and cluster work. Among the Navajo motifs are squash-blossom necklaces and crescent-shape pendants. Zunis are known for their combination of silver and stones. Zunis also produce fetishes, which are either polished stones that appear in the shape of a bear or carvings of wildlife (e.g., a snake) that are thought to contain a spirit.

The friars came to Arizona to spread the gospel and establish schools for Native Americans. They were instrumental in helping to create a written language for the Navajos, and there are displays in the museum of some of the original Franciscan translations. There are also photographs and exhibits depicting the friars' daily lives.

Next door is the wood and brick building that houses a statue called *The Redemption of Mankind, The American Pietà.* Ludwig Schumacher, born in Germany as the son of a Nazi, rejected his father's beliefs for a life of pacifism. He immigrated to America in the mid-1980s and settled in Arizona. A craftsman by trade and a sculptor by temperament, he found a section of a juniper tree that he wanted to carve into a representation of Michelangelo's Pietà. Unlike the original, Schumacher's is a vertical statue, standing 16 feet tall. It depicts Jesus being taken off the cross to where Mary waits.

If you take Route 264 east, you'll quickly arrive back at Window Rock. The **Navajo Tribal Museum and Gift Shop** (928–871–6673) and the **Navajo Arts & Crafts Enterprise** (928–871–4095) are located downtown next to the **Navajo Nation Inn** (800–662–6189). The museum houses intricate exhibits featuring life-size mannequins involved in tribal ceremonies and everyday activities. The arts and crafts enterprise is a Navajo organization that dates back to the 1940s. The purpose of this guild is to assure the quality, innovativeness, and authenticity of the crafts of its artisans. The guild also purchases arts and crafts from the Hopi, Zuni, and Santo Domingo tribes, so the selections here are very good. If you like Native American jewelry, make sure you see the Zuni pieces—especially the bracelets, which are for men as well as women.

At the one and only street light in Window Rock, take Route 12 north to **Tseghahodzani** (the Navajo name for "the rock with the hole in it"). This red sandstone landmark that gave the town its name is several stories tall, with a 130-foot hole in the center. There are picnic areas nearby, as well as the hogan-shaped council chambers where the tribe's eighty-eight council members meet four times per year. The chambers are open for self-guided tours.

One of the most spectacular sites on the reservation is **Canyon de Chelly** (928–674–5500; www.nps.gov/cach). Canyon de Chelly (*Shay*) is the scene of the final defeat of Navajo warriors who were holding out against troops commanded by General James Henry Carleton. In January of 1864, with one last battle that left twenty-three warriors dead, more than 200 Navajos surrendered. You can reach Canyon de Chelly by taking

Route 12 north along red-rock cliffs and past lush orchards. When you reach the junction for Route 7, take Route 7 (the backroad, some parts gravel) northwest to the town of **Chinle** (928–674–5500; www.south-westdirectory.com/chinle) at the western edge of *Canyon de Chelly* (about 50 miles). For an alternative route on which all the roads are paved, head west on Route 264, then north on Route 191 to Chinle. This route is about 80 miles. Follow the highway signs to the visitors center. The center has a museum that traces the history of Native Americans in the canyon. It also has an art gallery, demonstrations of Indian arts and crafts, and an information desk. Navajo guides can also be hired here.

At the visitors center you can also get a map that will show you the route of the rim drives. You can take these roads unescorted, though you will miss the most spectacular sights. If you want to experience the Canyon more fully, you must hire a guide who will take you on a hike or ride along with you in your four-wheel-drive (rentals include the guide). You get the benefit of a knowledgeable Navajo guide who can tell you the history and the lore of the valley, and you don't have to worry about accidentally sending your vehicle careering down a ravine. Cameras are permitted on these trips, and usually the guides

Exploring Canyon de Chelly

*W*hen you arrive at the entrance to Canyon de Chelly, the canyon walls are only about 30 feet high, but they eventually soar to 1,000 feet above the sandy floor. While in Canyon de Chelly, don't miss **Spider Rock Overlook.** Spider Rock is an 800-foot-tall chunk of sandstone about which there are many legends. In one Navajo version of a Bogey Man story, Navajo children are told by their parents that if they don't behave, Spider Woman— a demigod who also supposedly taught the Navajos how to weave—will take them away and leave them on top of the rock to die. Also be sure to see the **White House Ruins.** These remains of an 800-year-old Anasazi village were named for the white plaster used on one of the pueblo's walls. **Antelope House** is another set of Anasazi ruins that's worth a look. This more-than-90-room pueblo is located near a rock crevice where, in the 1920s, a mummy was recovered by archaeologists. The Anasazi sometimes wrapped their dead in ceremonial garments and placed them in hidden crevices where the weather and scavenger animals couldn't get to them. Mummies were found in the appropriately named **Mummy Cave,** also the site of a large set of ruins in the section of Canyon de Chelly known as **Canyon del Muerto** ("the canyon of the dead," so named because of burial sites uncovered here by archaeologists in the 1880s).

67

will pose for a picture provided you don't want to sell it to a photo stock agency or some such thing. Some guides will be willing to take you to villages where you can see jewelers and rug weavers at work and watch scenes of contemporary Navajo life. In some of these locations, you may be asked to leave your camera or sketch pad in the Jeep.

West of Canyon de Chelly, off Route 160, 20 miles south of Kayenta, lies the *Navajo National Monument* (www.nps.gov/nava). The 360 acres of the Navajo National Monument are beautiful pine forest containing the ruins of several Anasazi settlements. Stop at the visitors center (928–672–2366) 9 miles north of Route 160 on Route 564. Like most visitors centers on the reservation, there is an exhibit hall, an arts and crafts shop, and presentations on Navajo history. Best of all the center is next to an easy hiking trail that takes you to a view of the *Betatakin Ruins.* Betatakin, situated about 700 feet below the rim of the canyon, has about 135 rooms that were built sometime between A.D. 1200 and A.D. 1300. You'll need binoculars or a spotting scope to see much detail, but even from a distance they are impressive. You can inquire at the visitors center about ranger-guided tours to Betatakin, which include an exploration of the rooms themselves (involves some moderately strenuous climbing).

If you're feeling adventurous and want a truly off-the-beaten-path experience on the Navajo reservation, sign up for a horseback ride to *Keet Seel* (928–672–2366), a 160-room, well-preserved Anasazi settlement that's the largest cliff dwelling (in terms of total space) in Arizona. Keet Seel is only 8 miles from the visitors center, but the terrain is quite rough. During the summer months Navajo guides take about two dozen visitors at a time on horseback excursions to the settlement.

Don't leave the Navajo reservation until you've seen *Monument Valley* (928–871–6647), where countless Westerns, including John Ford classics like *Stagecoach,* were filmed. You can reach Monument Valley by driving north on Route 163. Though it straddles the Utah–Arizona border, most of the park is actually within Arizona. The nearly 30,000-acre valley spills across the landscape like a watercolor set of purples, reds, and golds. Jutting up at irregular intervals are tremendous mountains of sand-sculpted rock. The valley is unquestionably one of Arizona's most widely photographed sites, with its soaring sandstone monoliths and cliff formations that bear curious names like the Three Sisters and the Mittens. Many of the accommodations, such as *Gouldings Trading Post, Lodge and Museum* (801–727–3231), are located north of the Arizona border. The *Monument Valley Navajo Tribal Park Headquarters and Visitor Center* is also in Utah, about 5 miles past the state line off Route 163. Watch for the crossroads on Route 163, and take the one

Hogan at Monument Valley

that goes to the right. The visitors center offers dramatic views of Monument Valley. You can purchase a permit at the visitors center to take your vehicle on a rim drive of the valley, but the road is poorly maintained and bumpy. You'll have a much better time if you hire a guide at the visitors center to take you by Jeep or horseback on a tour of the full canyon.

One place that nearly everyone visits on the Navajo Reservation is *Four Corners,* the only place in the nation where four states (Arizona, Utah, Colorado, and New Mexico) converge. There's a marker at this point, and few Arizona vacations are complete without a photo of the travelers straddling this landmark. Four Corners is easily reached by taking Route 160 northeast.

There isn't an endless array of motels and eateries on the reservation, but of the few, most are well known and time-tested. In Kayenta the *Wetherill Inn* (928–697–3231) has fifty-four rooms, no restaurant or pool, but a small gift shop. About 10 miles away is the *Anasazi Inn at Tsegi Canyon* (928–697–3793), which is only a few minutes away from the Navajo National Monument and has great views. There's a twenty-four-hour restaurant and a gift shop but no pool. In Chinle the *Thunderbird Lodge Motel* (928–674–5841) has a cafeteria that's open until 9:00 P.M. and a gift shop. Canyon tours are also available through the motel.

For restaurants try *Amigo* (928–697–8448), off from Route 163 just north of 160; it serves Mexican, American, and Navajo cuisine.

Tucked entirely within the Navajo Reservation is the comparatively tiny 1.5-million-acre *Hopi Reservation* (928–734–2401), home to about

Inscription Rock

*O*ne place you're sure to want to visit on the Hopi Reservation is **Inscription Rock**. Take Route 264 east until it ends at the Keams Canyon Trading Post. After a 2-mile hike along Keams Canyon, you'll come to a dam. Nearby is a sandstone wall that bears the 1864 signature of Kit Carson. Carson, a buffalo hunter and sometime army scout, was the man General James Carleton ordered to deliver an ultimatum to the Navajos—that they must relocate to the Bosque Redondo reservation by the Pecos River or be destroyed.

9,000 people. This rocky terrain has been inhabited by the Hopi and their ancestors for hundreds of years. In fact the village of *Oraibi* on the third mesa (plateau) is the oldest continuously inhabited town in the United States, having been settled around A.D. 1100.

The reservation's villages are grouped on three separate mesas, with the *Hopi Cultural Center* (928–734–2401; www.psv.com/hopi.html) accessible from the first mesa off Route 264, about 5 miles west of the Route 87 junction. The center has a museum, a motel, a gift shop, and a restaurant with authentic cuisine. The motel's front desk staff is an excellent source for information about any tribal dances and ceremonies that the public may view. Though friendly, the Hopi closely guard their privacy and religious rituals. Some areas of the Hopi Reservation are open to tourists, whereas others are not. And although the Hopi do invite visitors to observe many of their colorful ceremonies, the use of cameras, video or audio recorders, and sketch pads is strictly forbidden. Hopi dances traditionally begin in December, with ceremonies stopping in July, but call ahead if you'd like to plan your visit to coincide with these events.

Wild West Country

*J*ust south of the Navajo reservation, near the junction of Route 77 and I–40, is the town of *Holbrook* (800–524–2459; holbrook chamb@cybertrail.com). About 100 years ago Holbrook was known as "the town too tough for women and children." Cowboys shot it out in saloons like the Bucket of Blood, and some of the killings associated with the Pleasant Valley War took place here. To get a look at what the town used to be like, drop by the old *Navajo County Courthouse* (800–524–2459; holbrookchamb@cybertrail.com) at 100 East Arizona

| Trivia |

Street. You can tour the sheriff's office and the jail and see exhibits depicting everything from the area's geologic history to an old-time barber shop. It's open 8:00 A.M.–5:00 P.M., Monday through Friday.

Arizona has its own "Triassic Park," actually the Petrified Forest National Park, where the remains of Triassic reptiles have been unearthed and ancient trees turned to stone 225 million years ago.

Once a year (usually in January) the town offers visitors a chance to obtain a very unusual souvenir: a letter delivered by the **Pony Express.** In commemoration of the area's history and as a kickoff to other festivities, a team of riders known as the **Hashknife Pony Express Riders** sets off from the Holbrook Post Office on a three-day trek to Scottsdale through the White Mountains. They carry thousands of letters with them, and each is canceled with a special mark that designates it as a Pony Express delivery. The riders' arrival in Scottsdale heralds the official kickoff of the city's annual Parada del Sol celebration. For more details about having a letter sent in this manner, contact Holbrook Postmaster, Pony Express Ride, Holbrook, AZ 86025.

For restaurants in Holbrook try the **Wayside Cafe** (928–524–3167) at 1150 West Hopi Drive (Route 66). It serves Mexican and American food Monday through Friday. The **Roadrunner Café** (928–524–2787) at 1501 East Navajo Boulevard [also Route 66] has sandwiches and specialties such as chicken-fried steak. Holbrook has no bed-and-breakfast inns but it does have more than 1,000 motel rooms, ranging from simple mom-and-pop–style lodging to more elaborate chain accommodations. *The Arizonian* (no, we don't normally spell it that way) *Inn* (928–524–2611) at 2508 East Navajo Boulevard has a pool and restaurant.

The **Petrified Forest National Park** and Painted Desert (928–524–6228; www.nps.gov/pefo/) are a short drive north from town on I-40. The **Painted Desert,** north of the freeway, provides vistas of green desert vegetation with mountains of red and purplish hues. If you're wearing polarized sunglasses, the effect can be quite striking. Conversely, if you're not wearing sunglasses, or if they're of the nonpolarized variety that don't block stray light, the scenery will look washed out and you'll wonder why you bothered to stop. If you plan to take pictures here, the same rule applies. If you can, use a polarizing filter on your lens or wait until the sun is at an angle, just after sunrise or just before sunset.

Across the road, the **Petrified Forest** is a marvel of the unique properties of nature. Littered across the landscape are giant chunks of what were once logs, part of a conifer forest that thrived millions of years ago. Long before humans walked the earth, the forest was covered by water, and sediments settled on the trees. Gradually, as the trees decayed, all that was left was hardened stone in the shape of the original tree. Because these fossils haven't been polished, you often have to look really hard to see the array of colors lurking in the stone.

Before heading off to see the sights, stop at the visitors center and grab a descriptive brochure. You'll probably want to see *Agate Bridge,* where a petrified log fell over a canyon. One story has it that more than 100 years ago, on a $10 bet, a cowboy rode his horse over that bridge—not a feat I'd care to duplicate! Another place to stop is *Newspaper Rock,* where ancient Indian tribes chiseled in all the news that was fit to chip.

By the way, it's illegal to remove any pieces of wood from the park, and, really, the stuff is so nice in the gift shops you'd be foolish to risk the fine. Stop by the *Jim Grays Museum* (928–524–1842) gift shop on Highway 180 at Highway 77, and you'll see many crafts made from petrified wood, as well as polished chunks of the material. Admission to the museum is free, and it's open 8:00 A.M. to 6:00 P.M. every day.

The Winslow area has long been inhabited, and Hopi archaeological remains in the nearby *Homolovi State Park* (928–289–4106) date back many hundreds of years. The park, located off I–40 via Route 87, sprawls over 4,000 acres at 4,900 feet and has campgrounds and hiking trails, some of which will take visitors to petroglyphs and an old Mormon cemetery. Two of the Hopi Anasazi sites are open to the public. Several other sites are still being excavated. In the past the park has held "dig days" when visitors were allowed to help with certain aspects of the research. Write to the park officials at HC63–Box 5, Winslow, AZ 86047 to see about such special events. Also worth a look are the exhibits in the *Hubbell Building,* another old-fashioned trading post that sells Native American arts and crafts.

Winslow (928–289–2434) itself, founded in 1881, has quite a history. Named for General Edward F. Winslow, president of the St. Louis & San Francisco Railroad, the community was raised on the three Rs: ranching, railroading, and Route 66. The *Old Trails Museum* (928–289–5861) at 212 Kinsley has displays of all three stages of the area's history, as well as artifacts from its Native American history.

For a peek at more history and a beer or two, drive over to *Minnetonka Trading Post* (928–289–2561), which once was part of a shack owned by the legendary Hashknife Ranch. The Hashknife Ranch was part of the Aztec Land and Cattle Company, in the 1880s one of the largest ranching enterprises in the Southwest. The front wall of the building is made of petrified wood. Today it's a popular honky-tonk for cowboys.

EASTERN ARIZONA

Not all the sites being excavated are as old as the Anasazi ruins at Homolovi. The remnants of **Brigham City,** a rock fort founded in 1876 by Mormon settlers near the banks of the Little Colorado River, are currently being unearthed and prepared for public display. You can view the work taking place from North Road, an access strip just east of the golf course. Access can be limited at times.

Aircraft aficionados may want to make the drive along Second Street to Highway 87 and out Airport Road to the **Winslow Municipal Airport** (928–289–2429), recently named after the famous pilot. This airport is unique because it has the longest runways in North America. In addition it was designed by Charles Lindbergh (on his honeymoon, no less!) and built by Howard Hughes. The airport saw extensive military use during World War II, and today you still may be able to see old planes there because it's a slurry base for converted bombers used in fighting forest fires.

No visit to Winslow is complete without a stroll over to the park to see **"The Corner."** The Glenn Frey/Jackson Browne song "Take It Easy"— recorded first by the Eagles on their debut album and later by Browne—recounts an incident that occurred on the corner of Second (actually Route 66) and Kinsley. Every year the town holds a "Miss Flatbed Ford" contest in honor of the famous song's lyrics. Winslow has even built a "Take It Easy" park on this corner, using the space created by a fire that leveled the old Winslow Drugstore. The park is designed to resemble a 1944 photograph of the corner, depicting a long, lean cowpuncher lounging against a lamppost and speaking to a shorter cattle driver. T-shirts of this scene are available for sale.

Winslow has attracted filmmakers as well as musicians. Oliver Stone came to town to film part of *Natural Born Killers.* The kickoff scenes were shot in the **Red Sands Bar,** which has been closed for years but was refurbished as a roadside diner just for the film.

One of the most exciting projects in Winslow in years was the renovation and reopening of **La Posada** (928–298–4366; www.laposada.org), a Fred Harvey hotel located by the Santa Fe Railroad tracks at 303 East Second Street. The hotel, a National Historic Landmark, is a 60,000-square-foot Spanish Mission–style palace designed by famed architect Mary Jane Colter and built in 1930 at a cost of more than a million

Trivia

In its heyday, Winslow's La Posada hotel housed such celebrity guests as Clark Gable and Carole Lombard, Douglas Fairbanks and Mary Pickford, Charles and Anne Morrow Lindbergh, Gary Cooper, Jimmy Durante, John Wayne, Howard Hughes, Will Rogers, Harry Truman, and Franklin Roosevelt, as well as Japanese royalty.

dollars; it was frequented by many celebrities. During World War II, as many as 3,000 troops were fed in the dining hall each day. It closed in 1958 as the result of declining rail travel. It has fifty rooms.

Winslow has many chain restaurants as well as cafes, such as the *Brown Mug* (928–289–9973) at 308 East Second Street. It is open every day but Sunday. The fifty-year-old *Highway Diner* (928–289–3629) at 2201 North Park Drive is also open every day but Sunday.

You won't find any bed-and-breakfast inns in Winslow, but the dozen-and-a-half motels range from simple to sophisticated. The *Adobe Inn* (928–289–4638) at 170 North Park Drive has an indoor pool and hot tub, as well as a restaurant that's open for breakfast, lunch, and dinner.

Apache and Mormon Country

The *Apache Sitgreaves National Forest* (928–333–4301; www.fs.fed.us/r3/asnf) is an impressive stand of vegetation (about two million acres) that ranges from about 3,500 feet in elevation to more than 11,000 feet above sea level. Flora and fauna from many diverse environments can be seen here. Three dozen campgrounds, several hundred thousand acres of wilderness or primitive area blocked to vehicles, and nearly 900 miles of trails are here for those who love hiking and camping.

Many small towns, including Heber, Show Low, Pinetop-Lakeside, and Alpine, lie within the forest boundaries, and quite a few others are within an hour's drive or less. Widely used by vacationers during ski season, this area is also a cool (well, mostly) summer retreat. Bluegrass festivals and other activities help to draw visitors from all over the country.

Incidentally, it's within this stand of forest that Travis Walton, who lived in the Heber area, claimed to have been abducted by a UFO on November 5, 1975 (an intriguing refutation of his story is presented in Philip J. Klass's *UFO Abductions: A Dangerous Game*). Walton's story was told in *The National Enquirer* and in the 1993 film *Fire in the Sky*, which was filmed around the area.

Settled in 1878, *Snowflake* (928–536–4331) was one of the first Mormon communities founded in Arizona. Believe it or not, it wasn't named after an ice crystal—rather, it was built by Erastus Snow and William J. Flake. Flake was responsible for the actual acquisition of the land. He bought the land from rancher James Stinson, only to discover it also had been given to the Santa Fe Railway, and then to the Hashknife Ranch.

Mogollon Rim Overlook

*I*ƒ *you visit the forest, be sure to take the* **Mogollon Rim Overlook** *trail, which is accessible from Highway 260. This easy, 1-mile hike through pine forest affords magnificent canyon views where you'll be tempted to sit, listen to the wind, and observe the squirrels. The squirrels seem to like watching people, too—just don't move too fast.*

Like many Mormon settlers in Arizona, Flake met with hostility regarding his religious beliefs and, in 1884, he was arrested for polygamy and spent some months in the gruesome Yuma Territorial Prison.

The town follows Brigham Young's City of Zion design—wide boulevards and neatly squared-off city blocks. Today in the downtown area, many of the original homes—ranging in style from Greek Revival to Victorian to bungalow— look exactly as they did one hundred years ago. You can take a self-guided tour of the exterior of the historic homes year-round. You can also arrange for an interior tour of several of the homes. To schedule a tour, call the Snowflake/Taylor Chamber of Commerce at (928) 536–4331. Every July the community celebrates its heritage with Pioneer Days, during which there are guided house tours by costumed Snowflake residents, parades, theatrical productions, and other events.

Situated along Route 191, *St. Johns* (928–337–2000; www.wmonline.com/cities/stjohns.htm), the Apache County seat, prides itself on having a major *Equestrian Center* (928–337–4517) located next to the airport. The center has facilities for cross-country competition, dressage, and other events; however, no riding rentals for visitors are offered here. Call to find out if any horse shows are scheduled during your visit to the White Mountains. The *County Museum* (928–337–4737) is also located here at 180 West Cleveland Avenue. Artifacts of the area's history and prehistory—including a 24,000-year-old set of woolly mammoth tusks— are on display. The museum is open 9:00 A.M.–5:00 P.M. daily. Guided tours are available upon request.

You can certainly be forgiven if you think the communities in the White Mountain region blend together. It's easy to forget which town is on what side of which lake. In simple terms, *Show Low* (888–746–9569; http://ci.show-low.az.us; the town was named after an 1875 card game that supposedly established the town's ownership) is to the west on Highway 60 and just south of *Fool Hollow Lake Recreation Area* (928–537–3680). The town of Pinetop-Lakeside is south of Show Low along Highway 260.

Trivia

Eastern Arizona is home to much of what is considered to be the world's largest stand of virgin ponderosa pine.

Sunrise Ski Resort (800–772–SNOW; www.sunriseskipark.com) lies to the southeast along Highway 273.

The entire **White Mountains Apache Reservation** (928–338–1230) area is loaded with recreational opportunities: lakes, streams, nature trails, golf courses, and even **Hon-Dah** (Apache for "welcome") **Resort Casino** (800–929–8744; www.hon-dah.com) on Highway 260 just south of Pinetop-Lakeside. Many of these enterprises are owned by the White Mountain Apache tribe, which has done a phenomenal job with developing visitor services while maintaining the natural look of the terrain.

One of their finest accomplishments is the **Sunrise Park Resort** (800–772–SNOW), Arizona's largest ski resort. Three mountains— Sunrise Peak (10,700 feet), Apache Peak (11,000 feet), and Cyclone Circle (10,700 feet)—comprise the skiable terrain, which is laced with sixty-five trails and served by modern, high-speed quad, triple, and double chairlifts.

Day lodges on each of the peaks provide food and full rental facilities for skis and snowboards. Additionally the one-hundred-room **Sunrise Resort Hotel** (800–554–6835) provides accommodations, whirlpool spas, and saunas just 3 miles from the base of the mountain. The season starts in early December and, weather permitting, runs through late March or longer. Because the resort has extensive snowmaking equipment, it isn't totally dependent on Mother Nature; on a sunny, warm day in Phoenix, you can hop in your car and in four hours or so be in the snow.

Raven Site Ruin

*I*f Native American prehistory interests you, you might enjoy knowing that Raven Site Ruin (928–333–5857), an 800-year-old Mogollon and Anasazi settlement that's undergoing excavation, is also near St. Johns. What's unique about this program of the White Mountain Archaeological Center is that from May through mid-October, you can sign up to take part in the digging for a fee. A daylong visit includes an orientation, excavation, lunch, and a hike to view ancient petroglyphs. You can also choose to ride horseback to the petroglyphs. The visitors center is open even when the digging season is over. The center has exhibits of pottery, tools, and other artifacts found at the site. It also has a gift shop with books about the Southwest history of Native Americans and arts and crafts created by Apache, Navajo, and Hopi artisans.

About 30 miles south of Hon-Dah on Highway 73 is **Fort Apache Historic Park** (928–338–1230). This historic piece of frontier and military history operated from 1870 to 1922. Its primary mission was to keep the peace between white settlers and northern tribes of Apaches. General Crook used the fort as a base of operations during his expeditions against Geronimo and Cochise. Today the fort is a museum, with many of its buildings intact, including officers' quarters, horse barns, and a cemetery. Among the exhibits on display in the new **Apache Cultural Center** (928–388–4625) are some on the history of the Apache tribe in Arizona.

You'll find many little cafes and family restaurants in the White Mountains. For lunch try **Annie's Gift Shop and Tea Room** (928–368–5737) in Pinetop-Lakeside.

There's little evidence of it now, but about 100 years ago **Springerville** (928–333–2123) was one of the toughest towns in the Arizona territory. Because the dense foliage of what is now the Apache-Sitgreaves National Forest provided so many excellent hiding places and made tracking difficult, a countless number of stolen horses and cattle ended up here. Even the tattered remnants of the Clanton gang, after an infamous shoot-out in Tombstone, decided to avail themselves of this area's greater tolerance of lawless activity.

The town's name is actually the result of the hard-luck nature of its early days. Henry Springer, a merchant, went broke attempting to help out some ranchers, and as an ironic twist the town founders decided to name it after him.

Springerville's history as a pioneer outpost is honored by being one of twelve sites in the nation to have a **Madonna of the Trail Statue.** These statues, made of algonite stone that incorporates Missouri granite to

Round Valley Ensphere

*T*here's another unusual, albeit modern, structure you may want to take a look at: the $11 million **Round Valley Ensphere.** Located 2 miles south of Springerville in the nearby town of **Eagar** (928–333–2123; www.az.tourist.com) this dome looks a bit like something out of The Jetsons and boasts the distinction of being the first domed high school stadium in the country. Built in 1992, the dome is 440 feet in diameter and covers a total floor area of 189,000 square feet. Besides a football field, the dome can accommodate up to seven removable basketball courts. It also has tennis courts and 5,000 seats.

achieve a glowing hue, were placed on points along the National Old Trails Road by the Daughters of the American Revolution in the late 1920s. The statue depicts a sturdy, stoic pioneer woman in homespun clothes, cradling one child in her left arm and holding a rifle in her right, while another child clings to her skirts. To find the statue, drive down Main Street to the post office; the Madonna is directly across the street.

About 2 miles north of town is *Casa Malpais* ("house of the badlands") *Pueblo Archeological Park* (928–333–5375; www.casamalpais.com). This Hopi and Zuni ruin and National Historic Park was first reported by an archaeologist in 1883. Stone walls, pottery, and other features of the site indicate that it was occupied for several hundred years before being abandoned in the fifteenth century. Some areas related to the site remain off-limits to the public, but there's still plenty to see, including a museum on Main Street in Springerville and a field laboratory. Lectures and tours are conducted on a frequent basis. For more information write to Casa Malapais Pueblo, P.O. Box 390, Springerville 85938.

The tiny towns of *Greer* and *Alpine* (fewer than 1,000 residents total) have some visitors services, including quaint lodges and cabins, but most shops and restaurants in the area are in Springerville. For a quick meal, try *Booga Reds* (928–333–2640) at 512 East Main Street, which offers homemade Mexican and American food from 5:30 A.M. until 9:00 P.M. every day. (The name, by the way, is a nickname given to the owner by an old cowboy.)

Motels, guest ranches, and cabins are spread throughout the White Mountains area, including *The Paisley Corners B&B* (928–333–4665) at 287 North Main Street, Eagar, and the *Tal Wi-Wi* ("where the sun rises first") *Lodge* (928–339–4319) in Alpine. The Tal Wi-Wi Lodge, incidentally, features some suites that have fireplaces and hot tubs.

Henry and Tonto

If you take Highway 260 west from Show Low, you'll travel a scenic route through the Apache-Sitgreaves National Forest, across the Mogollon Rim and down into the Tonto National Forest. There are many small towns along the way in which you can stop for gas and travel supplies. The area also features scads of National Forest campgrounds and developed hiking trails. Within a few hours you'll reach *Payson* (928–474–4515), only about 90 miles from the major metropolitan area of Phoenix, yet close to immense stands of ponderosa pine and numerous lakes and streams. As you might expect, this small

Down to the Water in Rafts

*L*ike amusement park rides that warn expectant mothers and those with back problems not to ride, I half expected the warning of "you will get wet" to be little more than hype when reading the brochure from Desert Voyagers Guided Raft Tours. But after receiving countless paddle-splashes of water, soaking my reporter's notepad, and turning my sneakers into sponges, I accepted it as a statement based solely on fact. The water in the Gila River is very wet.

Most adventurers immediately think of the mighty Colorado River when their thoughts turn to a rafting adventure, but Arizona's wet and wild offerings don't stop there. Sure, the bulk of the white-knuckle, Godzilla-sized rapids are in the Grand Canyon, but other waterways—including the Salt, Verde, and Gila Rivers southeast of the Phoenix metro area—offer calmer, yet extremely pleasurable rafting excursions.

As a solo passenger on my trip, which departed from a site near the town of Winkleman, I was elected captain of the raft. That dubious honor put me in charge of six other rafters—a family of four from Wisconsin and a young Scottsdale couple—and gave me the prime seat at the back of the craft. While coaching my paddlers was a cinch, garnering any respect from them was a major challenge—one that ultimately led to mutiny and my trip overboard into the chilly waters of the Gila, notepad and all.

On the way, though, our platoon of four rafts encountered one rapid, spectacularly rugged scenery, and wildlife like great blue herons. According to our guide, the Gila is a historically important river, having once divided Mexico from the United States. Desert Voyagers, based in Scottsdale, is one of more than twenty companies that offers raft, dory, and kayak trips on Arizona's rivers. They can last from as little as my half-day adventure of a few miles to as many as nineteen days, covering the entire 277 miles of the Grand Canyon.

A complete list of river rafting companies can be obtained from the Arizona Office of Tourism.

community of about 9,000 is a recreational stop for people on their way to the White Mountains, as well as a vacation spot for world-weary warriors from the Phoenix area.

Nature trails, campgrounds, and various frequent festivals keep this area active. In August Payson is the location of the ***World's Oldest Rodeo.*** In September the ***Fiddlers' Contest*** brings the region's finest pickers and fiddlers to the pine country. October is time for the ***Great Payson Jerky Jamboree,*** which tests the skills of jerky makers using everything from beef to elk. In October a regional ***fine arts festival*** is held here, and in December, Payson kicks off the holiday countdown by lighting ***Christmas trees at the Swiss Village.*** The ***Swiss Village Shopping Plaza*** is at the southern tip of town. It is a small collection of gift shops, restaurants, and a hotel, the *Inn of Payson* (928–474–3241). Though rather touristy, the shops have some interesting handmade European items, and the Alpine-style village is an unusual sight in the midst of an Arizona forest.

Just north of here up Highway 87 is the *Tonto Natural Bridge State Park* (928–476–4202; www.pr.state.AZ.us/parkhtml/tonto.html), a limestone formation that's believed to be the largest such formation (400 feet long) in the world. A bit farther north are the tiny mountain towns of *Pine* and *Strawberry* (928–474–4515). The *Strawberry Schoolhouse,* built in 1884, is the oldest standing one-room schoolhouse in the state. It held its last classes in 1907, and today it's a historic state monument that's open for tours on the weekends.

Globe (800–804–5623), a town of about 6,000, is a mining community with strong links to Arizona's past. You can reach Globe by driving south on Highway 87 to Highway 188, which soon becomes Highway 88 beyond the Tonto National Monument. Continue south on this scenic route through the pines of Tonto National Forest, and you'll soon enter Globe. From the Phoenix area, it's an easy jaunt east on U.S. 60. In the downtown area, more than two dozen historic buildings date from just before the turn of the twentieth century until the late 1920s. They range in style from territorial adobe to Queen Anne Victorian. You can drop by the *Gila County Historical Museum* (928–425–4385)—the former Globe-Miami Mine Rescue Station, built in 1920—at 1330 North Broad Street, on U.S. 60 next to the Chamber of Commerce to look at exhibits of how the community grew and changed. The museum is open daily 10:00 A.M.–4:00 P.M. Also worth a look is the town's *Cobre* ("copper") *Valley Center for the Arts* (928–425–0884), in the building that used to be the Gila County Courthouse. It has been lovingly restored as a venue for the Copper Cities Community Players and also houses visual arts studios. You can take a self-guided tour and browse in the gift shop, which sells everything from handpainted furniture to stationery. The center is open Monday through Saturday 10:00 A.M. to 5:00 P.M., and Sunday 12:00 P.M. to 5:00 P.M. Donations are gratefully accepted.

Follow Broad Street through Globe for about 1.5 miles, and you'll see a clearly marked road leading to *Besh-Ba-Gowah* ("metal house") *Ruins* (928–425–0320). This Salado pueblo settlement was built around A.D. 1225 on top of what was once a Hohokam pit house. The site has been restored to allow visitors a self-guided tour. You can climb around in the ancient settlement using ladders to follow the same paths original occupants took to get to the roof or down to the first floor. An on-site

Besh-Ba-Gowah

museum houses artifacts retrieved from the excavation, including the world's largest single-site collection of Salado pottery. Admission is $3.00 for adults and $2.00 for seniors. Children ages 11 and younger are free. It's open from 9:00 A.M to 5:00 P.M.

After you've worked up an appetite crawling in and out of the pueblo, try a homestyle meal at *Judy's Cook House* (928–425–5366) in Globe. Refreshed, you can prowl Globe's half-dozen or so antiques or gift shops, such as *Turquoise Ladies* (928–425–6288) at 996 North Broad Street.

As for accommodations, several bed-and-breakfast inns in Globe provide rest for the weary. *Cedar Hill* (928–425–7530) at 175 Cedar Hill is an early twentieth-century wooden home built by one of the area's most influential families. Antiques (including a queen-size brass bed) have been used in furnishing the rooms, and amenities like cable TV in the living room help you feel comfortably at home. Call for current rates. A relatively new—but very old—find is the *Noftsger Hill Inn* (928–425–2260), a bed-and-breakfast that has guests sleeping in the actual classrooms and janitor's closet of the old Noftsger Hill School at 425 North Street. Owners Pamela and Frank Hume have been lovingly restoring the property since purchasing it in 1991 and have five rooms currently available—all furnished in "comfortable antiques."

Arguably the best reason to visit the *Safford* area is to drive up Swift Trail to the summit of *Mount Graham Discovery Park* (928–428–6260; www.discoverypark.com), a 10,720-foot peak in the Pinaleno Mountains known as a "sky island," as its lofty green peak appears to be a lush island hovering in the clouds. This mountain has had an interesting history over the years. About 100 years ago when there was a fort nearby, injured soldiers were taken up Mount Graham to recuperate in the pine-scented air. For a number of decades there have been cabins, Christmas tree farms, and campgrounds on the mountain. The park is open Tuesday through Sunday and costs $4.00 for adults.

More recently the University of Arizona and the Vatican have each built telescopes on the peak. The University of Arizona has an international reputation for its astronomical research, which has been based at several locations in southeastern Arizona. The Vatican's involvement in celestial research dates back to the time of Galileo. Together the university and the Catholic church were able to create telescopes on Mount Graham whose data augment each other's. The Mount Graham telescopes have thrilled astronomers because the scopes are on the cutting edge of technology, but they have angered some environmentalists, who feel the vehicular traffic created by the telescope projects threatens the already endangered Mount Graham red squirrel. University of Arizona biologists are monitoring the squirrels for potential negative impact. To date, there are no signs that the observatory construction has negatively affected the squirrels.

The telescopes aren't visible from the ground, and indeed they are all but invisible in the forest (on a visit to the site, I couldn't detect them until I was only a few hundred yards away). They also are off-limits to anyone without an official U.S. Forest Service permit, which keeps unwanted traffic off the final dirt road to the top where the squirrels live.

Although you can't drive up Swift Trail to where the scopes are, there are many beautiful areas on the mountain where you can pull off and have a picnic. There are also several scenic overlooks where you can see gorgeous, sweeping vistas of the valley all the way down to Safford. If hiking is on your agenda, there are nine major trails on Mount Graham. One of the best is the moderately difficult 14-mile Round the Top Mountain Trail, which meanders through shady pine forest and also offers some good views of the countryside. Visit the Safford-Graham, County Chamber of Commerce (1111 Thatcher Boulevard, Safford, AZ 85546) for detailed hiking maps. Whenever you visit Mount Graham, bring a jacket, because it's chilly even in the summer.

As an aside, on your way up Swift Trail you'll pass a *Federal Penitentiary* on your left where Watergate conspirator John Ehrlichman was imprisoned for a while.

About a half-hour drive to the south, along State Route 266 off Route

191, is the town of **Bonita** (no chamber of commerce). Like a lot of Arizona towns, this one can claim a rather wild and woolly heritage. Bonita's old, two-story general store is no longer open; it was formerly known as George Atkins' Saloon. Right out front on August 17, 1877, Francis P. Cahill, a strapping Irish laborer, picked a fight with a youngster known as Henry Antrim. He called Antrim a pimp. Skinny, bucktoothed Antrim—a known horse thief and ne'er-do-well—was no match for Cahill. When the big man rushed him, the eighteen-year-old kid pulled a pistol and gut-shot his tormentor. Cahill died the following day, and the boy who went on to be called William H. "Billy the Kid" Bonney chalked up his first kill. Some stories dispute this and insist that Billy began killing in another state at the age of twelve, but it seems likely that those tales are the sort of tabloid fabrications that were rampant in Victorian times (some things don't change).

From Bonita it's a quick drive north to **Fort Grant,** the site of an even more infamous frontier tragedy. In March 1871, about a half-mile outside what was then Camp Grant, lived a settlement of several hundred Apaches—mostly women and children—who were under the care of the camp's commander, Lt. Royal Whitman. Though the camp seemed peaceful and Whitman had reason to be optimistic about future relations between the Apaches and the U.S. government, a group of men from Tucson, including some civic leaders, held the opposite view. On April 28 they rode out from Tucson with a force of about 100 Papagos and Mexicans to attack the Apache camp in retribution for previous Indian raids, which actually had nothing to do with the Camp Grant Apaches.

On the morning of April 30 the raiders leveled the peaceful Indian camp, slaughtering all the inhabitants. In the aftermath, Whitman and his troops buried the dead and tried to assure other Apaches in the area that the U.S. army had not played a part in the massacre. President Grant ordered the Arizona territorial governor to find the men responsible for the carnage. The leaders of the raid were brought to trial in Tucson, but all were acquitted. Today Fort Grant is a penitentiary, and there are no visitor services.

For more information on the original Camp Grant story, check the **Graham County Historical Society** (928–348–0069) archives located in the old high school in Thatcher, which has exhibits detailing the frontier history of Graham County.

PLACES TO STAY IN EASTERN ARIZONA

HOLBROOK
Motel 6,
2514 East Navajo
Boulevard, 86025;
(928) 524–6101.
Moderately priced motel-style lodgings with a swimming pool and a laundry.

KAYENTA
Holiday Inn,
Junction U.S. 160 and
163, 86033;
(928) 697–3221,
fax: (928) 697–3349.
Modern facility, conveniently located near Monument Valley. *Remember:* Navajoland is alcohol-free!

PAYSON
Days Inn & Suites,
301-A South Beeline
Highway, 85541;
Motel with fireplace, pool
with spa pool, pets OK.

PINETOP-LAKESIDE
Woodland Inn,
458 East White Mountain
Boulevard, 85933;
(928) 367–3636.
Motel-type accommodations with continental breakfast and in-room coffee. Pets OK with a $10 fee.

Rainbow's End Resort,
Route 2, Box 1330, 85929;
(928) 368–9004.
Charming accommodations on Rainbow Lake.

SHOW LOW
Days Inn,
480 West Deuce
of Clubs, 85901;
(800) 329–7466,
fax: (928) 537–8692.
Newly renovated, full-service, 122-room inn with in-room refrigerators and microwaves. Free buffet breakfast.

TUBA CITY
Quality Inn,
P.O. Box 247, 86034;
(928) 283–4545.
On the Navajo Reservation.

WINSLOW
Days Inn,
2035 West Highway 66,
86047;
(928) 289–1010.
Near the interstate with restaurants and gas stations nearby.

PLACES TO EAT IN EASTERN ARIZONA

HOLBROOK
Kentucky Fried Chicken,
1629 East Navajo Boulevard, 86025;
(928) 524–3179.

All-American fried chicken in a fast-food format.

PAYSON-PINE-STRAWBERRY
Ponderosa Steak House,
404 East Highway 260,
85541;
(928) 474–4995.
Steaks and other full meals—family dining.

PINETOP-LAKESIDE
Christmas Tree Restaurant,
P.O. Box 1617, 85929;
(928) 367–3107.
Posh dining among the pines. This curiously named eatery was a long-time favorite of the late humorist Erma Bombeck.

Charlie Clark's Steak
House,
P.O. Box 1283, 85929;
(928) 367–4900.
Consistently good food and service for true carnivores. Look for the horse on the roof!

WINSLOW
Arby's Roast Beef,
2121 North Park Drive,
86047;
(928) 289–5565.
Beef sandwiches are the specialty—fast food.

Web Sites for Eastern Arizona

Arizona Office of Tourism's Web site,
www.arizonaguide.com,
has links to Web sites for the following cities:

Holbrook, Show Low, and Pinetop–Lakeside.

Central Arizona

The Valley of the Sun and Phoenix

The *Valley of the Sun* cuts a diagonal swath from Wickenburg in the northwest to Florence in the southeast with Arizona's primary gateway, *Phoenix Sky Harbor International Airport,* located almost exactly in the center and encircled by the major interstate highways that provide access in every direction, to every region of the state. Covering approximately 2,000 square miles of the *Sonoran Desert,* the Phoenix metro-plex is made up of twenty-two separate cities and towns, the best-known of which are Phoenix (the core city), Scottsdale (best known for its resorts and art galleries), and Tempe (home of Arizona State University and excellent coffee shops). Gaining in popularity and in recognition are Mesa and Apache Junction in the east valley, Florence and Casa Grande to the south, and Glendale (known for its antiques shops) and Wickenburg (billing itself as the dude ranch capital of the world) in the west valley.

For information about the Valley of the Sun, your best starting point is the *Phoenix Convention and Visitors Bureau* (602–254–6500 or toll-free 877–225–5749, www. phoenixcvb.com) at One Arizona Center, Phoenix. When you get to town, the CVB also has a downtown walk-in information center that is open Monday through Friday from 8:00 A.M. to 5:00 P.M. at 50 North Second Street.

If you were born to be wild and you're looking for a unique way to see the Valley (or even the rest of Arizona), you may want to contact *Western States Motorcycle Tours* (602–943–9030 or AZMcRent@aol.com) at 9401 North 7th Avenue, Phoenix. The company offers experienced riders the opportunity to climb aboard a Harley-Davidson or a BMW bike and take off on an adventure. The company's owner, Frank Del Monte, has done that himself, and he can either offer you advice on where to ride or arrange a guided tour for groups of five or more riders.

Central Arizona

CENTRAL ARIZONA

AUTHOR'S TOP PICKS

The Arizona Center

Arizona Science Center

Heard Museum

Rawhide

Bank One Ballpark

Phoenix Zoo

Desert Botanical Garden

Grady Gammage Memorial Auditorium/ASU

Orpheum Theatre

Mill Avenue—Downtown Tempe

Phoenix is the sixth largest city in the nation, with more than 1.2 million residents within city limits and about 2.8 million total in the greater Phoenix area. Towns spread out along I–10 and I–17 like strands of a giant spider web, covering the Valley of the Sun with attractions that are sure to ensnare travelers. The Valley is made up of a myriad of pseudo-, micro-, and full-scale communities, and it can be quite daunting to find your way around if you don't have a detailed map. To the west of Phoenix are the suburban communities of Sun City West, Surprise, El Mirage, Youngtown, Sun City, Peoria, Glendale, Buckeye, Wickenburg, Litchfield Park, Goodyear, and Avondale. To the east are Paradise Valley, Scottsdale, Tempe, Mesa, and Apache Junction. Farther south are Guadalupe, Ahwatukee, Chandler, Gilbert, Sun Lakes, Higley, Queen Creek, and Casa Grande. And that's just a partial list!

Gliding over the desert in a hot-air balloon is an interesting way to travel off the beaten path; so is doing it yourself with a parasail or sailplane (aka glider). Flying adventures are available in several corners of the Valley. For glider flights *Arizona Soaring/Estrella Sailport* (928–568–2318 or 602–821–2903, twenty- four hours) is located south of the city, in Maricopa, a short drive off I–10. They offer rides and instruction seven days a week from 11:00 A.M. weekdays, 9:00 A.M. weekends. Northwest of the city is *Turf Soaring School* (602–439–3621; www.turfsoaring.com) at the Pleasant Valley Airport in Peoria. They are open every day from 9:00 A.M. to 5:00 P.M. Hot air balloon rides are available from *Unicorn Balloon Company* (480–991–3666 or 800–468–2478), which launches from Scottsdale Airport, and *Hot Air Expeditions Inc.* (480–502–6999 or 800–831–7610), which launches from a site in North Scottsdale. Early morning is the traditional time to balloon, and Hot Air Expeditions makes it an occasion available year-round with a champagne breakfast catered by Vincent Guerithault, chef of a well-known Phoenix restaurant, Vincent's on Camelback. HAE also does a sunset trip during the winter months with champagne and hors d'oeuvres catered by Chef Vincent (who does a mean chocolate truffle, by the way). Also offering balloon flights—plus jeep safaris, parasailing, horseback rides, and raft expeditions—is *Adventures Out West* (602–996–6100 or 800–755–0935; www.adventuresouthwest.com). They also offer combination Jeep-balloon trips (one with a western breakfast option) and may give a

Top Annual Events in Central Arizona

January

Litchfield Park: West Valley Native American Invitational Fine Arts Festival. *150+ Native American artisans (602–935–6384).*

Phoenix Arizona Stock Show and Rodeo. *State Fairgrounds (602–258–8569).*

Various locations: Annual Phoenix Open. *One of the PGA Tour's top events, with the finest golfers in the world (602–870–4431).*

February

Wickenburg: Gold Rush Days. *Senior rodeo (50+ years old), gold-panning, carnival, western dances, arts and crafts, BBQ, gem show, mucking, and drilling (928–684–5479).*

Apache Junction: Arizona's Renaissance Festival. *Sixteenth-Century European Village (520–463–2700). (February and March)*

Apache Junction: Lost Dutchman Days. *Includes professional rodeos, gold panning (480–982–3141).*

Casa Grande: O'Odham Tash. *Largest all–Native American rodeo, arts and crafts (520–836–4723 or 800–916–1515).*

Phoenix: Native American Hoop Dance Championship. *Heard Museum—top Native American dancers from the United States and Canada (602–252–8840).*

Mesa: Arizona Scottish Highland Games *(602–431–0095).*

Scottsdale: All-Arabian Horse Show. *Two thousand of the world's most beautiful Arabians, Half-Arabians, and National Show Horses (800–877–117).*

March

Chandler: Ostrich Festival. *Ostrich races and big-name entertainment (602–963–4571).*

Phoenix: Annual Jaycees Rodeo of Rodeos. *Nearly seventy years old—traditional rodeo and concert (602–254–6500).*

Phoenix: Heard Museum Guild Annual Indian Fair and Market. *Features more than 300 of the nation's top Native American artists (602–252–8840).*

Phoenix: Standard Register Ping LPGA Tour Event. *Top women golfers in the world (602–495–4653).*

Picacho Peak: Civil War Battle Re-Enactment *(520–466–3183 or 602–542–4174).*

Scottsdale: Arts Festival. *Rated among the top in the country (800–877–1117).*

Tempe: Old Town Tempe Spring Festival of the Arts. *Second largest arts and entertainment festival in the Southwest (800–283–6734).*

April

Glendale: Gaslight Antique Walk. *Seventy-five stores, specialty shops, and restaurants stay open from 6:00 to 9:00 P.M. third Thursday of the month (623–930–2960).*

Scottsdale: Culinary Festival. *Great Arizona Picnic, Le Tour Culinaire (800–877–1117).*

May

Mesa: Cinco de Mayo Fiesta (800–283–6372).

Rock Springs: Sweet Onion Festival. Onion seeds, fresh veggies and onion, onion recipe books, onion recipe contest (602–470–8086).

June

Phoenix: Grand Canyon State Summer Games. Olympic-style competition in twenty-two different sports. Athletes of all ages and abilities, with one category available for elite athletes (602–517–9700).

Scottsdale: Summer Rodeo Series (800–877–1177).

July

Scottsdale: Summer Spectacular Art Walk (800–877–1117).

Tempe: Downtown Cooldown. Featuring twenty tons of snow (480–921–2300).

August

Scottsdale: Bring in the Clowns. The largest clown gathering in the Southwest (800–877–1117).

September

Wickenburg: Fiesta Septiembre. Desert Caballeros Western Museum—arts and crafts, folklorico dancers, mariachi bands, mercado, salsa contest (928–684–5479 or 684–0977).

October

Phoenix: Cowboy Artists of America Sale and Exhibition (602–257–8382).

Tempe: Tostidos Fiesta Bowl Duck Race. 70,000 rubber ducks, $100,000 in prizes (480–350–0900).

November

Ahwatukee: Foothills Festival of Lights. Horse-drawn hayrides to luminaria hike on South Mountain (480–898–7900).

Chandler: Tumbleweed Tree Lighting Ceremony and Parade of Lights. Nutcracker performance, crafts, games, and Santa (602–786–2518).

Fountain Hills: Fountain Festival of Arts and Crafts (480–837–1654).

Glendale: Celebration of Art. Outdoor street festival (623–930–2960).

Mesa: Arizona Temple Christmas Lighting. Five hundred thousand plus lights in the garden and a lighted reflection pool (602–964–7164).

Scottsdale: Thunderbird Balloon Classic. Continuous entertainment, 130 balloons (800–877–1117).

Tempe: Fantasy of Lights. Downtown illuminated, city tree lighting, fireworks, multiple live entertainment stages (480–894–8158).

Wickenburg: Bluegrass Festival and Fiddle Championship. (928–684–5479).

December

Phoenix: Pueblo Grande Indian Market. Native American artisans, traditional foods (602–495–0901).

> **Phoenix: Las Noches de las Luminarias.** *Desert Botanical Gardens—7,000+
> lit luminarias line the garden pathways, musical groups perform (480–941–1225).*
> **Phoenix: Zoo Lights.** *Phoenix Zoo—600,000+ lights, lighted animal exhibits
> (602–273–1341).*
> **Tempe: Fiesta Bowl Block Party.** *Thirty-plus musical groups on five different stages,
> pep rally (800–635–5748).*
> **Wickenburg: Cowboy Christmas, Cowboy Poets Gathering.** *Desert Caballeros
> Western Museum—poetry, ballads, stories, singin', and storytellin' (928–684–5479).*

discount on the other activities they offer. As a guideline to prices, flights with Adventures Out West range from $79 to $185 per person.

The Global Group (623–877–9350; www.fly/in/america.com) based in Glendale offers air cruises to key statewide attractions (e.g., Grand Canyon, Monument Valley, Bisbee). Their international staff can provide tours in eight different foreign languages—Afrikaans, Chinese, Dutch, French, German, Japanese, Korean, and Spanish. Also based in Glendale is *Arizona Professional Air Travel* (623–933–7590), another flight tour offering Arizona flightseeing to key state attractions—plus they have a forty-five-minute champagne and souvenir photo flyover of the Greater Phoenix area.

Jeep tours are another great way to see the desert. Two companies operating in the Valley of the Sun are *Desert/Mountain Jeep Tours* (480–860–1777), which offers a choice of five four-hour itineraries and operates twice a day, seven days a week, and *Desert Storm Hummer Tours* (602–922–0020), which gives you three to four hours in one of those double-wides that are billed as the most powerful four-by-four vehicles on earth.

Phoenix emerged from the ashes of Hohokam settlements, prospector claims, and military camps around 1850. It was long an agricultural center, diverting water from the Salt River to irrigate many acres of farmland. In true colorful Western fashion, the man most credited with envisioning the irrigation potential of the Valley was Jack Swilling, a drug-addicted Confederate deserter who led the Battle of Picacho Pass (more on this later in this chapter). Today you can still see mini-farms, even within the built-up areas of the city. Probably the biggest contrast between the Valley of the Sun and other areas in central and southern Arizona is that Phoenix and its environs are much greener, with sizable lawns, countless public parks, and many nonnative trees.

Bank One Ballpark Fun Facts

- BOB's retractable roof has six operable telescoping panels that, when open, provide 5.25 acres of open sky.
- The roof is driven by two 200-horse-power electric motors that consume between $1.20 and $2.00 worth of electricity to open or close the roof.
- The park has 650 television sets, 81 concession stands, and 580 bathroom stalls.
- Using as much cooling power as 2,285 average homes, the 8,000-ton air-conditioning system takes about four hours to lower the temperature inside the stadium from 110 to 72 degrees.
- About 17,000 tons of structural steel was used to build the park.

All this greenery provides some much-needed summer shade. Many areas of the Southwest are hot during the summer, but Phoenix has the reputation as a true hot spot, with 100-plus-degree temperatures the norm throughout the summer. As miserable as that may sound, particularly to those from the north, the area's nearly nonexistent humidity—coupled with the zillions of swimming pools that dot the landscape—makes it relatively bearable even in the dead of summer. Even locals will talk about soaring highs of 115 and 120, but thankfully, those days are as rare as snow in the desert.

Sports fans may want to begin their exploration of the Valley at the home of the National Basketball Association's Phoenix Suns, as well as the Women's National Basketball Association's Phoenix Mercury, the American Football League's Arizona Rattlers, and the National Hockey League's Phoenix Coyotes. The Arena is also one of the best places in the Valley to see musical performers, ice shows, rodeos, and whatever. *America West Arena* (602–379–7878; www.americawestarena.com) can be found at 201 East Jefferson Street. The exit is well marked from I–17 North, and once you find Jefferson Street, just keep your eyes peeled for the giant basketball mural. The arena is the modern, gray brick building on the opposite side of the street. Several businesses within the arena cater to fans and tourists. On the first level, the *Teamshop at America West Arena* (602–514–8321) sells posters, key chains, wearables, and other items related to the Suns and other Phoenix-area teams. *The Platinum Club* restaurant (602–379–7777) on the second level serves lunch Monday through Friday and also remains open during events. New to the Phoenix skyline is the *Bank One Ballpark* (www.bankone-ballpark.com) or "BOB" as it's nicknamed. Even when

It's a Cool 100° Outside

*A*ccording to the National Climatic Data Center's summer heat stress index comparison, Phoenix's low humidity results in more comfortable summer weather than most would imagine. Although the outdoor temperatures average 100.5 degrees fahrenheit, it feels like it's only 96. Compare that with Dallas, where the average high may be only 93, yet high humidity makes it feel more like 109.

the Arizona Diamondbacks aren't playing, this massive, $350-million, retractable roofed stadium is worth seeing—perhaps over lunch at *Friday's Front Row* (602–462–3503), a casual eatery built right into the stands that's open daily. Here, too, you can shop for sports memorabilia at *Teamshop at Bank One Ballpark* (602–462–6700). As an aside, BOB is the first ballpark ever to be built with its own swimming pool off right field. Only in Phoenix!

Just north of America West is *Majerle's* (Mar-leez) *Sports Grill* (602–253–9004) at 24 North 2nd Street. This is the place that Suns' former star Thunder Dan Majerle built with his phenomenal three-point shooting ability. Besides being a great pub and restaurant (with menu items named after the players and probably the best french fries available anywhere), the grill is packed tighter than an overstuffed gym bag during Suns' games, when you can watch the action on a projection TV. Hours here are 11:00 A.M. to 1:00 A.M. daily. Another popular spot that has sprung up within walking distance of the sports and entertainment venues is *Leinenkugel's Ballyard Brewery* (602–462–3800) at 201 South 4th Street.

The biggest news in food and nightlife in Phoenix in years has been the opening of *Alice Coopers'town Phoenix* (602–253–7337) at 201 East Jefferson Street by the legendary hometown boy and rock star known as Alice Cooper. Basically a sports and music bar, Cooper'stown is located near the America West Arena/Bank One Ballpark. The menu features barbeque and waitpersons sport the Alice Cooper trademark teardrop. Also near the sports venues with an equally sports-oriented format is the 24,000-square-foot *Jackson's on 3rd* (602–254–5303) at 245 East Jackson Street near 3rd Street.

Your best bet to sample the variety of nightlife Phoenix offers is the classy downtown complex called *The Arizona Center.* Located between 3rd and 5th Streets north of Van Buren, it's a complete dining, shopping, and entertainment complex. There's the new *AMC Arizona*

Center 24 Theatres, a twenty-four-plex movie theater (602–956–4AMC) that shows first-run features in their full digital sound splendor and offers reduced ticket prices for the early shows. Also on the ground level is *Player's Sports Bar & Grill* (602–252–6222), which has six big screen TVs surrounding the bar as well as TV sets in every booth. Upstairs is *Phoenix Live!* (602–252–6222), which covers three-quarters of the northern part of the complex and offers a choice of nightlife formats on weekends. At one end is *Ltl' Ditty's,* a dueling-piano bar where a team of performers pull in crowds with their hysterically funny and often irreverent lyrics and a clap-along/sing-along performing format. In the middle is the pool hall and bar area and at the other end is *Decades* for dancing to hits from the 1970s, 1980s, and 1990s on a small raised dance floor. Also on the second level of the Arizona Center is *Moondoggies Tourist Trap & Beach Bar* (602–253–5200), a spacious retro-dance club that's open Wednesday through Sunday nights.

For concert lovers, *Cricket Pavilion* (602–254–7200) at 2121 North 83rd Avenue offers about three dozen events per year, including most of the top pop/rock and country acts that tour Arizona. The Pavilion, which seats about 20,000 under the stars, has provisions for video screens and adjacent areas for booths that sell everything from bottled water to concert tees to margaritas. During major events such as Jimmy Buffett's annual visit, the Pavilion turns into Party Town, with a forest of colorfully decorated Parrotheads—which is what Buffett fans call themselves—bopping to the tunes.

A Musical Spawning Ground

*P*hoenix is well known as a stepping stone to the recording mecca of Los Angeles. Over the years this city has given the world the Tubes, jazz/pop vocalist Rickie Lee Jones, and Francine Reed (a gospel/blues vocalist who recorded with Lyle Lovett). The Valley's most memorable contribution to the music industry is probably glam/heavy-metal/shock-rock god Alice Cooper. Alice (aka Vincent Furnier) attended Cortez High School (8828 North 31st Avenue, Phoenix, AZ 85051), if any of you rock fans want to see where this self-styled bad boy got his start. Together with his band, the Earwigs, he first recorded in the Valley on the Santa Cruz label. Away from the stage, he lives a quiet life north of Phoenix in beautiful Paradise Valley. He plays golf and has, on occasion, dispensed advice to local bands. At one time he owned a Native American art gallery in Scottsdale.

You can find great restaurants at the 3rd and 5th Street's answer to shopping and entertainment: *The Arizona Center.* You'll find familiar formats at *Pizzeria Uno* (602–253–3355), *Hooters* (602–495–1234), and *Fat Tuesdays* (602–256–2444). You'll also find local favorites: *Mi Amigo Mexican Grill* (602–256–7355), *Sam's Café A Southwestern Grill* (602–252–3545), and *Lombardi's* (602–257–8323) for wood-fired pizza and Italian seafood specialties. For something quicker and cheaper, the Arizona Center also has a food court on the second level that's open weekdays 10:00 A.M. to 9:00 P.M., Saturday to 10:00 P.M., and Sunday 12:00 to 6:00 P.M., with everything from pizza by the slice at *Scotto's Pizza* (602–256–6460) and hand-mixed ice cream at *Cold Stone Creamery* (602–257–0226) to sandwiches by *Subway* (602–257–9080) and fruit drinks by *Sun Valley Smoothies* (602–253– 6771). *Diego's Mexican Grill* (602–716–5878) is another option.

The Valley is a great place to hear up-and-coming musical acts, and as you might expect, there are a lot of hip clubs. Your best bet for finding the hot new spots in town is to look for one of three local freebie publications distributed from street stands and in local restaurants and shops. *The Rep* and *Get Out* are published by the local newspapers; another source is *New Times,* a fairly hefty read that does a good job covering the Valley's nightlife.

They may have built this city on sports and rock and roll, but art and architecture also offer significant appeal. Several key buildings were designed, built, or influenced by master architect Frank Lloyd Wright; some of them are private residences, but four are public buildings that can be toured. The most impressive is *Taliesin* (Welsh for "shining brow") *West* (480–860–2700; www.franklloydwright.org/03TALIESINS/west. html) at 12621 Frank Lloyd Wright Boulevard, Scottsdale. Built against the foothills of the McDowell Mountains just outside of Scottsdale, this winter retreat was begun in 1937 by Wright, who made many changes to it over time (the original structure used canvas flaps instead of glass windows). Today it's the headquarters of the Frank Lloyd Wright Foundation, which operates a school of architecture as well as maintaining an archive of the master's designs. Taliesin West has a gift shop and offers tours that range from a one-hour overview to an in-depth, behind-the-scenes study. Special events at the site include desert walks and nighttime city-light gazing.

Wright also had an influence on one of Phoenix's best-known resorts, the *Arizona Biltmore* (480–955–6600) at 2400 East Missouri, which at one time was run by the Wrigley chewing gum family. Though most believe that the resort was designed by Wright, it was actually at the hand of his former apprentice, Albert Chase McArthur. The story goes that McArthur invited the famous architect to oversee construction of the hotel, which he did quietly for a few months before completely removing himself from the project. Nevertheless, Wright's touch can be seen in the block structure of the resort as well as in its distinctive spire. You have to be a guest to get a guided tour, but you're welcome to look around the lobby and other public areas.

If you're still looking for the "Wright stuff," drop by *Grady Gammage Memorial Auditorium* (480–965–6678; www.asupublicevents.com) on Apache Boulevard and Gammage Parkway in Tempe. This structure, on the grounds of Arizona State University, was actually begun after Wright's death and was completed in 1964. The circular building has been extensively praised for its physical beauty as well as its acoustics. Tours are conducted during the academic year from September through May, and the center regularly hosts touring Broadway groups that perform such hits as *Cats, Phantom of the Opera,* and *Beauty and the Beast* to sold-out crowds.

Last on a tour of Wright structures would be *The First Christian Church* (602–246–9206) at 6750 North 7th Avenue, Phoenix, which could perhaps win an award as the Frank Lloyd Wright building completed most posthumously. Though this slant-roofed structure with its repeated triangular motif was drafted in 1950, construction didn't take place until 1970. In any case, the design is breathtaking. Tours are available by special arrangement.

Architecturally, *Downtown Phoenix* has a lot to admire. The copper-domed landmark that used to be the *State Capitol* building (602–542–4675; www.lib.AZ.us;clickonmuseum) at 1700 West Washington Street is now a historical museum. (The actual government offices now

DASH around Downtown Phoenix—It's Free!

*W*hether your reason is tired feet or summer heat, the **DASH (Downtown Area Shuttle)** *is the easy way to see downtown Phoenix. These orange and purple minibuses run every six to twelve minutes from 6:30 A.M. to 6:00 P.M. They take you past—or near—all the major downtown hotels, restaurants, theaters, and sights, including Heritage Square, the*

Arizona Science Center and Phoenix Museum of History, Bank One Ballpark, and the Arizona Center. Plus, in the middle of the day (11:00 A.M. to 2:00 P.M.) the route is extended to include the State Capitol, the Mining and Mineral Museum, and the Hall of Fame. Best of all, DASH is free. Look for a stop where you see the signs with a dashing jackrabbit.

occupy the modern, nine-story tower that rises behind the historic dome.) You can wander about at your own pace, or take one of the guided tours to peer into exhibits on the state's political past. Also worth a look in the downtown area are Heritage Square, St. Mary's Basilica, and the Old County/City Hall complex.

The Heritage Square complex (602–262–5029) at 7th and Monroe Streets is a group of historic houses and buildings, museums, boutiques, a bistro, and a gift shop/tearoom surrounding a cool, green courtyard. The *Arizona Doll and Toy Museum* is located here, as are the Phoenix Museum of History, the Arizona Science Center, and the *Victorian Rosson* and *Silva Houses.* For a bite to eat you can drop by the *Teeter's Tea Room,* or for dinner, *Pizzeria Bianco* (602–258–8300). Hours vary on the various attractions, and some are closed during the summer, so call ahead to avoid disappointment.

The *Arizona Science Center* (602–716–2000) at 600 East Washington is the kind of place where Carl Sagan would have felt right at home. Now located in a new $47-million building just east of the Phoenix Convention Center, the facility is a hands-on (and in some cases, whole-body-on) learning complex that encompasses Arizona's largest planetarium, a wide-screen theater, and 350 interactive exhibits that beg to be touched and explored.

The Old County Courthouse

*N*o tour of the downtown area is complete without a look at the **Old County Courthouse** on Washington Street between 1st and 3rd Avenues. The county structure, thought to be the largest terra-cotta–surfaced structure in the state, is a grand old courthouse built in the late 1920s. On the second floor is the courtroom where the famous Miranda trial took place. The 1963 case, involving Ernesto Miranda, who was arrested for a rape that occurred near Bethany Home Road and 17th Street in Phoenix, threw a harsh spotlight on police interrogation tactics and resulted in the Miranda Rights ruling ("You have the right to remain silent. If you give up the right to remain silent . . . ").

Ironically, the building also played a key role in one of Clint Eastwood's cop films. In The Gauntlet, Eastwood plays a Phoenix policeman who has to provide protection for a witness. In the film's climax Eastwood drives a bus through downtown Phoenix and runs it up the steps of the Old County Courthouse. The structures in the County/ City complex are public buildings; as such they are open to visitors, but no tours are offered.

Next door is *The Phoenix Museum of History* (602–253–2734) at 105 North 5th Street, between Washington and Monroe where interactive exhibits highlight territorial and early statehood days in Arizona and emphasize the multicultural heritage of the state.

Arizona is known as the Copper State. It produces more than 65 percent of the nation's domestic supply.

St. Mary's Basilica (602–252–7651) at 231 North 3rd Street is a soaring edifice that seems out of place, yet is oddly natural amid all the new downtown structures. Built in 1881, it is the oldest Catholic church in the city and a popular place for weddings and other major events. If there aren't any services taking place when you visit, you can walk around inside and marvel at the various forms of architecture that were used in constructing this Phoenix landmark (call for hours). It also, interestingly enough, has its own gift shop selling religious articles and mementos.

The *Herberger Theater Center* (602–252–8497) at 222 East Monroe is an understated earth-tone structure that provides space for eight performing arts groups—including the very popular (and deservedly so) Arizona Theatre Company, which uses professional actors from stage and screen to perform original and time-tested works in Phoenix and Tucson. The company's season usually runs September through May.

Along Washington Street en route to the State Capitol you'll find two small off-the-beaten-path museums worth considering. The first at 1101 West Washington and 11th Avenue is the *Arizona Hall of Fame Museum* (602–542–4675); the other is the *Arizona Mining & Mineral Museum* (602–255–3791) at 1502 West Washington and 15th Avenue, which honors the industry that built Arizona and made it the number-one mining state in the country for nonfuel production. You'll see turquoise, smithsonite, wulfenite, malachite, azurite, and pyrite; you'll also see some gold.

If you're hungry after a downtown tour, a great place to eat is *Tom's Tavern* (602–257–1688), centrally located on the corner of Washington and 1st Avenue. Seating is indoors and out (with misters in the summertime), and the politically driven menu offers sandwiches named after local office holders, past and present. Hours are 7:00 A.M. to 8:00 P.M., Monday through Friday. For breakfast, lunch, and dinner, check out *Kricket's* (602–258–3411) at 401 North 1st Street in the downtown Ramada Inn. Kricket's is decorated with photographs and other memorabilia that reflect the city's past, and it offers American and Southwestern cuisine.

Another choice in the neighborhood is at *Seamus McCaffrey's Irish Pub & Restaurant* (602–253–6081) at 18 West Monroe.

While you're downtown, be sure to get a look at the Spanish Colonial–style *Orpheum Theatre* (602–252–9678 for tours; 602–262–7272 for tickets) at 203 West Adams. Built in 1929, the theater was used for films and vaudeville performances. Mae West and W. C. Fields both graced this stage. Following an exhaustive, meticulous $14-million restoration project, the Orpheum reopened in early 1997. Broadway road shows play here.

Before leaving central Phoenix the *Heard Museum* (602–252–8848) is an Arizona "must-see" located at 2301 North Central near Monte Vista Road. Long known for its vast collection of Native American art, both the exhibit space and the parking area have been recently expanded to allow more visitors more ways to appreciate the craftsmanship and design abilities of the Native Peoples of the Southwest. Barry Goldwater's collection of hand-carved katsina dolls is there; so is the doll collection of the Fred Harvey Corporation. Also fascinating to see and study are baskets, jewelry, pottery, and textiles. The artist-in-residence program gives you a chance to meet and hear artists discuss their work; plus, you can see replicas of traditional Indian dwellings including a Navajo hogan, an Apache wickiup, and a Hopi corn grinding room.

There's a two-fer waiting to be discovered at Phoenix's Papago Park, and they're side by side on Galvin Parkway east of downtown. *The Phoenix Zoo* (602–273–1341) at 455 North Galvin Parkway is the only zoo in the country that is 100 percent privately funded; it's spacious, neat, and amusing, which is why it's also regarded as one of America's finest. Designed as a series of habitats, it includes an African veldt, a South

America's Heros: Phoenix's Firefighting Museum

*A*mong the many unusual places to visit in Phoenix is the largest firefighter museum in the world. The **Hall of Flame** *(602–275–3473; www.hall offlame.org) at 6101 East Van Buren has almost one hundred antique and classic fire engines as well as firefighting artifacts of all types. The fire engines date as far back as 1725 and* are as new as 1961. One of the carriages was used to fight the 1871 Chicago Fire. Photos, artwork, badge and arm patch displays, and even a fire safety exhibit for kids round out the items of interest here. Admission is $5.00 for adults. It's open 9:00 A.M. to 5:00 P.M. Monday through Saturday, and 12:00 to 4:00 P.M. Sunday.

American rain forest, and a traditional Arizona farm. Docents and teen volunteers make the exhibits come alive, and a Disney-style tram covers the entire complex. Two worthwhile special events during the year are "Boo at the Zoo," when children visit wearing Halloween costumes; during the holidays, "Zoo Lights" is a must-do. It's a month-long celebration (early December to early January) when the trees and the cacti are lit every evening until 10:00 P.M. and mimes, magicians, and carolers appear in the central courtyard or on the pathways. The zoo is open 364 days of the year (closed only December 25); hours are 9:00 A.M. to 5:00 P.M. except in summer (May 1 through Labor Day) when hours are 7:30 A.M. to 4:00 P.M. Next along the road is *Desert Botanical Garden* (480–941–1225) at 1201 North Galvin Parkway home to one of the world's largest and most diverse collections of desert plants as well as fine examples of Native American housing styles. It's a great place to learn more about cacti and their nasty habits before you set off on a desert hike; it's also an eye-opener to the beauty and delicacy of desert wildflowers, bushes, and small trees. Events here during the year include spring and fall plant sales, Music in the Garden, Jazz in the Garden, and, like its neighbor the zoo, there's a winter holiday celebration of lights called "Las Noches de las Luminarias" each year. The Botanical Garden is open every day except December 25; hours are 7:00 A.M. to 8:00 P.M. May through September, and 8:00 A.M. to 8:00 P.M. October through April.

The *Arizona Hall of Fame Museum* (602–255–2100) at 1101 West Washington is devoted to exhibits about people of the state who have become known. As their leaflet says, this includes the famous, the not yet famous, and even the infamous. The museum may be easily visited through use of the free DASH buses.

North on Central Avenue from downtown is the *Phoenix Art Museum* (602–257–1880; www.phxart.org) at 1625 North Central at McDowell Road, which houses a wide ranging collection of art works, including American, European, Spanish Colonial, Latin American, and Asian paintings and sculptures. Of particular interest to visitors may be their collection of Western American works featuring the works of Southwestern artists. Children will enjoy both the ArtWorks Gallery—a hands-on, "brains-on" activity room for children—and the Thorne Miniature Rooms, which show how people lived during historic periods in the United States and Europe.

The *Phoenix Public Library* (602–262–4636) at 1221 North Central Avenue is an exceptional research and reading resource. The building also is of architectural interest. You can also see exhibits there relating

Finding an Address in Phoenix

*T*he Greater Phoenix area is built in the Western tradition of squares. It's exactly 1 mile from one main road to the next, often with a semimain thoroughfare at the halfway point. The only thing that stands in the way of this perfect patterning is the buttes and mountains that pop up here and there in the Valley of the Sun. Finding an address east to west is fairly simple. The numbering begins at Central Avenue and moves logically and predictably either west through the avenues or east through the streets, so you know that 2400 East Camelback is at 24th Street or 4300 West Indian School is at 43rd Avenue. North-South addresses are not as simple—numbering begins at Washington Street downtown, but you have to know that Camelback Road is 5000 North. Similarly, when you get into other towns in the Phoenix metro area, you'll find they too have a 1st Street or a 5th Avenue and in some cases—Scottsdale or Tempe for example—it's the roads running north–south that are named and some of the east-west streets that are numbered. Go figure! And be sure you know which city you're in, because numbering starts again—and goes town by town—when you get into what's called the East Valley (see below). Here's a bit of help with some of the more well-traveled thoroughfares in the Greater Phoenix area:

Street or Road Name	Numbers Begin At
Washington	0 North/South (1000 North in Tempe)
Van Buren	300 North
Roosevelt	1000 North
McDowell	1600 North
Thomas	2900 North
Osborn	3400 North
Indian School	4100 North
Camelback	5000 North
Lincoln	6600 North
Glendale	7000 North
Northern	8000 North
Shea	10600 North
Thunderbird	13800 North
Bell/Frank Lloyd Wright	17000 North
Pinnacle Peak	23400 North
Southern	6000 South (3300 South in Tempe; 1200 South in Mesa)
Elliot	10800 South (7600 South in Tempe; 3000 South in Chandler)
Ray	14000 South (1000 South in Chandler; 1600 in Gilbert)

to city life in Phoenix. One not-to-be-missed example of cooperation among residents is the library's centennial quilt, which hangs in the central area of the first floor near the children's book section.

One of the Valley's most unusual attractions is the *Mystery Castle* (602–268–1581) at 800 East Mineral Road near South Mountain Park in Phoenix. This eighteen-room stone structure, which also incorporates wire rims from a Stutz Bearcat, was put together completely by hand. The mystery comes from the fact that the builder never told his family about the work. He had always promised his daughter that he would build her a castle, and one day he left their home in Seattle and came to Phoenix to undertake the project. She only found out about the castle when his will was read, and she lives there to this day. The castle has thirteen fireplaces, lots of antiques, and the general sense of being smack dab in the midst of somebody's dream. You can tour this unique home Thursday through Sunday from 11:00 A.M. to 4:00 P.M. October through May only. The cost is $5.00 for adults.

The *Pioneer Arizona Living History Museum* (602–465–1052) at 3901 West Pioneer Road on I–17, 1 mile north of Carefree Highway, is a group of more than two dozen buildings, some authentic, and some reproductions that are used by reenactors to re-create the image of the frontier West. Visitors can see metalworking, dressmaking, carpentry, and other activities going on just as they were more than one hundred years ago. Open Wednesday through Sunday, 9:00 A.M. to 5:00 P.M. October to June only.

The *Pueblo Grande Museum* (602–495–0901; www.pueblogrande.com) at 4619 East Washington is an actual Hohokam village that was abandoned around A.D. 1450. The museum's exhibit rooms have permanent displays of artifacts and also serve as a venue for workshops such as pottery making and archaeology. Hikes to nearby ancient petroglyph sites are also a featured event. For almost twenty years the museum also has held an annual Indian market (usually in December), where more than 500 artists sell their works. The market also features traditional music and dancing, food, and beverages.

If you're in the mood to shop during your trip to Phoenix, you're in luck—the Valley is flush with shopping centers. One of the first, and still one of the best, is the west side *Metrocenter* (602–678–0017) at 9617 Metro Parkway (at I–17 off Peoria Avenue). A sprawling complex of more than 200 shops and restaurants, it also boasts a multiplex theater, an indoor arcade, and an outdoor amusement park. The whole complex is surrounded by hotels and eateries.

Mystery Castle

Another cool place to shop is the *Biltmore Fashion Park* (602–955–8401; www.shopbiltmore.com) at Camelback and 24th Street. The shops here aren't joined by enclosed corridors, but the inner court is shaded, so it's pretty comfortable year-round. There are boutique-style shops, nationally known retailers such as Macy's and Saks Fifth Avenue, plus Williams Sonoma, Ann Taylor, Gucci, and Border's Books and Music, among others.

A themed eatery just across the street, where the trademark Fender guitar shape heralds your arrival, is the *Hard Rock Cafe* (602–954–0613) at 2621 East Camelback Road. The restaurant displays mucho memorabilia, including instruments and costumes donated by musicians. Outdoor seating is available, illuminated by an unusual flame-spouting fountain.

Scottsdale and Its Neighbors

Scottsdale, as a community, began in 1888 when Army chaplain Winfield Scott purchased land to grow citrus and other crops. Over the years the town has emerged as a world-renown resort destination, offering great shopping, public parks, nationally recognized museums, frontier-type attractions, and galleries galore.

In fact Scottsdale is *loaded* with galleries. In at least three separate areas—Main Street Arts and Antique District, Marshall Way, and Fifth Avenue Shopping Area (in which there are more than 200 specialty shops)—you can stroll for hours and get a close-up look at everything from traditional Native American arts and crafts to nineteenth-century fine art. You can easily walk or take Scottsdale's local transportation—a trolley—to these various areas, but you may want to take your car, because you'll no doubt buy something!

Lovena Ohl Gallery (480–945–8212) at 7144 Main Street represents emerging and established Native American artists, with Katsinas, pottery, paintings, and other works. *American Fine Art Editions, Inc.* (480–990–1200 or 800–466–8276) at 3908 North Scottsdale Road, represents the contemporary art scene very well with an eclectic collection of original work by internationally acclaimed twentieth-century artists (Neiman, Wyeth, Picasso). *Borgata* at 6166 North Scottsdale Road is a Mediterranean-style complex of about forty-five shops and eateries, with cobblestone paths, fountains, towers, and all the ingredients of a fairy-tale setting (albeit one that takes plastic!). If all the shopping makes you hungry, wander into *Cafe Terra Cotta* (602–948–8100), a nouvelle style, informal yet sumptuous place created by restaurateur Donna Nordin (who was named by PBS as one of the great chefs of the Southwest) and her husband Don Luria. The cuisine, well flavored and tailored to Arizona tastes, is very moderately priced, and menu selections include everything from vegetarian items to seafood to fare that leans toward more traditional continental offerings.

Cosanti and Cause Bells

*I*n addition to the architectural work of Frank Lloyd Wright that is so much a part of the Phoenix-Scottsdale landscape, you'll also want to try to see the more fantastical and futuristic work of Italian architect Paolo Soleri. **Cosanti** (480–948–6145; www.cosanti.com) at 6433 Doubletree Ranch Road, Scottsdale, is an example of his concept of blending desert landscaping with earth-formed concrete structures. Everywhere you walk among the courtyards, terraces, and gardens, there are bronze and ceramic windbells tinkling. Designed by Soleri and his artisans, these Cause Bells, as they are known, represent national and global issues. You can watch them being made; you also can buy them to provide funding for the various organizations that work on solving world problems. Cosanti is open 9:00 A.M. to 5:00 P.M. Monday through Saturday and 11:00 A.M.–5:00 P.M. Sunday. The foundry is open to the public in the morning—it's best to call first. Donations accepted.

If you're staying at a hotel or resort way north in Scottsdale you'll be glad to know there are art museums within reach. Located in a corporate complex, the *Fleischer Museum* (480–585–3108; www.fleischer.org) at 17207 North Perimeter Drive near Pima and Bell Roads is devoted to American Impressionism, aka California School. Or if your wandering takes you north to Carefree, you will also find an extension of the *Heard Museum* of Native American art and crafts located in the El Pedregal Marketplace on Scottsdale Road and Carefree Highway (for information call the main museum at 602–252–8848).

When you tire of shopping, take a drive out to *Rawhide* (480–502–1880) at 23023 North Scottsdale Road, Scottsdale. It's a re-created 1880s frontier town, complete with shoot-outs and melodrama; stagecoach, camel, and burro rides; and a number of Old West restaurants and shops.

About 12 miles east of Scottsdale is the community of *Fountain Hills.* Fountain Hills can be reached by taking Shea Boulevard east through the desert foothills until it runs into Fountain Hills. Besides being home to the *Tallest Fountain in the World* (560 feet, as verified in the *Guinness Book of World Records*), this picturesque town has a number of local sights that are worth a look. *Out of Africa Wildlife Park*

A Carefree Life

*A*bout twenty minutes north of Fountain Hills are the twin communities of Cave Creek and Carefree. **Cave Creek** was a mining community one hundred years ago, and over time it has become a diverse town of a little more than 3,000 residents. Nearby **Carefree** is a bedroom community that began development in the 1950s and today serves as home to famous faces such as news anchor Hugh Downs and actress P. J. Soles (*Halloween, Carrie, Rock and Roll High School*). Carefree also is the location of the largest, most accurate sundial in the Western Hemisphere. This impressive timepiece, which sweeps out of the earth like a giant scimitar, can be found off Cave Creek Road and Sunshine Way. One stop you should definitely make in Carefree is **el Pedregal** (*"the place with many stones"*) (480–488–1072; www.elpe dregal.com) at 34505 North Scottsdale Road. This Morrocan-influenced marketplace has clothing stores (including several Western boutiques featuring the ultrahot retro forties ranch-wear look), gift shops, and several eateries. The inner courtyard is used for music and dance performances, as well as visual arts events. The center is also home to the Heard Museum North (623–488–9817), a satellite facility of the acclaimed downtown Phoenix Native

el Pedregal

(480–837–7779) showcases big cats and offers a popular attraction, their daily Tiger Splash show, that involves staffers swimming with white tigers and other ferocious felines. More wildlife—the casino gaming variety—is found just up the road at the **Fort McDowell Casino** (800–THE–FORT; www.fmcasino.com), where visitors challenge Lady Luck twenty-four hours a day, seven days a week; there's a free shuttle, if you need it. **Saguaro Lake,** an artificial reservoir on the Salt River, offers a number of boating, waterskiing, and swimming opportunities, as well as a steamboat paddle wheeler (602–837–3060) that does regular tours and dinner cruises. You can reach Saguaro Lake by taking Highway 87 north until you reach Bush Highway. Head south on Bush Highway, and it will take you to the lake.

While you're in Fountain Hills, drop by for a bite at **Que Bueno** (602–837–2418) at 11883 North Saguaro Boulevard. This Mexican restaurant has won plaudits for its homemade salsa and features savory desserts like chocolate chimichangas.

The West Valley and Wickenburg

On the western side of the Valley—accessible by heading west out of downtown Phoenix on I–10—is the tri-city area of Avondale, Goodyear, and **Litchfield Park.** Litchfield Park sprang to life as a company town in 1916 when Goodyear Tire and Rubber executive Paul Litchfield purchased the land to use as a cotton farm back in the days when cotton cords were utilized in automotive tires. Today the town is best known as the location of *The Wigwam Resort* (800–327–0396 or 623–935–3811; www.wigwamresort.com) at 300 Wigwam Boulevard. This four-star resort is composed of charming adobe casitas that were initially built for Goodyear officials. The Wigwam is especially favored by golfers because it features three eighteen-hole golf courses. Two of these, the Gold Course and the Blue Course, were designed by well-known golf-course architect Robert Trent Jones Sr. The Gold Course, which was selected by *Golf Digest Magazine* as one of the top seventy-five courses in America, is a whopping 7,100 yards long. Because of the Wigwam's off-the-beaten-path location, it also offers guests amenities such as horseback riding and trap and skeet shooting.

Not surprisingly for an area that was raised by the rubber giant, nearby *Avondale* is home to *Phoenix International Raceway* (623–252–2227), the location of the world's fastest paved 1-mile oval track. The raceway attracts huge crowds; famous drivers such as Mario Andretti, Emerson Fittipaldi, and Al Unser Jr.; and brings hundreds of millions of dollars into the tri-city coffers.

Northwest of Metropolitan Phoenix

At the junction of Routes 93 and 60, *Wickenburg* is a frontier town that's been a popular getaway destination for decades. Within a half-dozen or so miles there are five guest ranches that offer dudes and dudettes a close-up glimpse of the cowboy way of life. Because of this concentration of lodges serving the "City Slicker" set, Wickenburg has earned the title as "The Dude Ranch Capital of the World."

Prospector/farmer Henry Wickenburg, a native of Prussia, founded the town some 130 years ago after discovering the largest gold-producing strike in the history of the state. He called his mine the *Vulture Mine.* If you're interested in viewing the remains of Wickenburg's mining camp, it's about a dozen miles from town. Drive about 2.5 miles west of Wickenburg on Highway 60, turn left onto Vulture Mine Road, and continue. The pavement will end, and you'll be on a dirt road that can be a bit bumpy (don't attempt this drive during or immediately after a rainstorm). For most ordinary vehicles, the farthest you'll be able to continue on this road is about 4 miles. When you pull off the road, you'll see Vulture Peak, a tall hill with a crease in the middle of its summit. Vulture Mine is just to the southwest of the peak.

The remains of the wood and adobe buildings that once made up the

Vulture camp can still be explored. Though the mine mostly dried up around the turn of the twentieth century, some limited excavation is still being carried on in the area. Be careful to confine your explorations to buildings and hillsides that aren't marked as private property.

Mining is no longer a major portion of Wickenburg's economy. The lovely scenery, which ranges from creosote bush and cacti to oak and pine trees, draws visitors; and ranching and agriculture have helped to keep the city's coffers well stocked.

If you drive in from the west off U.S. 60, you can continue on the roadway that becomes Wickenburg Way, center of many of the area's hotels and restaurants. U.S. 89–93 also leads into the town; once in the town limits, it's called Tegner. Either way, it's easy to get around, and most of Wickenburg's attractions are in the downtown center grid.

There's a lot of history in this town, including many buildings that date from the turn of the twentieth century or earlier. One of the most interesting is the **Hassayampa Building** near Apache and Frontier. Originally built as a hotel for railroad passengers, it had nine separate fireplaces and a huge kitchen. Today it's office and shop space. Other locations worth stopping by to have a look at include **Hyder's Livery Stable** across the street from the Hassayampa Building. The stable, with its distinctive rock wall, is much classier than the simple barn-like buildings you generally see in Western towns. When it ceased being a stable in the 1920s, it was turned into a garage and auto dealership. The **Upton House** on Washington Street, west of Apache Street, was built from locally produced bricks. It was once occupied by one of the wealthiest families in the area.

Nearby on Frontier Street and Wickenburg Way is the **Desert Caballeros Western Museum and Park** (928–684–2272) at 21 North Frontier Street. The museum displays modern artwork from members of the Cowboy Artists of America in addition to pieces by American masters

The Code of the West

*I*f you're fascinated by the "Code of the West" (as is nearly anybody who grew up watching The Rifleman *and* Wanted: Dead or Alive*), head for the Circle K store in Wickenburg near Teg-* ner and Wickenburg Way. Behind the store is a 200-year-old **mesquite tree,** known as the "jail tree," which was used from 1863 to 1890 as a place to chain miscreants before the town had a jail.

Trivia

"Hassayampa" is actually an Apache word that means "river that runs upside down." Oddly, the preserve is one of the few locations where the river does not run underground.

like Frederic Remington. There are also period rooms depicting Wickenburg's early years. The small park adjacent to the museum features a life-size statue by Joe Beeler of a cowboy kneeling beside his horse. The museum and museum store are open year-round, Monday through Saturday, 10:00 A.M. to 5:00 P.M. and Sunday 12:00 to 4:00 P.M. Closed major holidays.

Wickenburg is better known for its current hospitality than for its earlier law enforcement policies. Its guest ranches range from a cozy, historic hacienda to an elaborate resort that has its own golf course. Among these is **Rincon Ranch Lodge** (928–684–2328 or 888–684–2338), operated by the Mule Show Outfitters of Glacier National Park as a B&B that also offers trail rides from two hours or a full day with lunch. **Rancho Casitas** (928–684–2628) is closed during the summer and has separate cottage-style houses with kitchens and fireplaces. It also has a pool and horseback riding facilities. **Kay El Bar Ranch** (928–684–7593 or 800–684–7583) is a traditional adobe guest ranch with a pool and horseback riding; it is open mid-October to May 1. **Flying E Ranch** (928–684–2690) is an actual working cattle ranch that also has a tennis court, pool, spa, and sauna; its season is November to May. **Rancho de los Caballeros** (928–684–5484 or 800–684–5030) caters not only to horse lovers but also to tennis buffs and golfers; it is open from October to May. Entertainment-industry mogul Merv Griffin's **Wickenburg Inn Tennis & Guest Ranch** (928–684–7811) has a variety of planned activities, including tennis clinics, an arts and crafts program, and a nature center. It is open all year.

In keeping with Wickenburg's frontier history, area restaurants include steakhouses and several establishments serving Mexican fare, but you also can find Chinese cuisine, fish and chips, and several cafes that have home-cooked specialties. **The Horseshoe Cafe** (928–684–7377) at 207 East Wickenburg Way has American cuisine and is open daily year-round from 5:00 A.M. to 2:00 P.M. **March Hare** (928–684–0223) at 170 West Wickenburg Way features homemade baked goods, salads, stews, and sandwiches. It is open year-round, Tuesday through Saturday from 9:00 A.M. to 2:00 P.M. Another cool hangout is **Screamers** (928–684–9056) at 1141 West Wickenburg Way, a 1950s-style diner named after the owner's daughters—I swear I'm not making this up! Screamers features a variety of dishes, including chicken, fish, hamburgers (even a Hawaiian Burger), hotdogs, and more. They're open daily from 10:30 A.M. to 9:00 P.M.; on Friday and Saturday they stay open until 10:00 P.M.

CENTRAL ARIZONA

A must-see attraction is the *Hassayampa River Preserve* (928–684– 2772), about 4 miles southeast of town on Highway 60. The preserve, managed by the Nature Conservancy, is a refuge area for birds like the zone-tailed hawk and the yellow-tailed cuckoo. It's not unusual to see the white posteriors of mule deer as they frolic through the brush. You may also see tracks made by raccoons, bobcats, and mountain lions. The preserve's office is in a restored home that once belonged to a group of settlers who fell victim to the Indian wars in the 1880s. Guided walking tours of the area are available at no charge, though it's suggested that visitors make a $5.00 donation.

Ghost towns are scattered throughout this rugged area, including Stanton, where prospectors are said to have picked up gold nuggets the size of potatoes, and Congress, home of a legendary tunnel that led from the general store to the town's hotel. Hidden Castle Hot Springs, east of Wickenburg, was at one time an exclusive spa where soothing natural hot spring water provided therapeutic relief for an impressive guest list that included President John F. Kennedy.

The city of *Glendale* (623–930–2960) has some delightful off-the-beaten-path surprises to offer. Best known locally as Arizona's antiques capital, a recent expansion of the *Old Town Glendale* antiques shopping area has turned some of the former craftsman bungalo-style homes of nearby *Catlin Court Historic District* into shops and restaurants (streets and alleys are gaslit in the evenings every third Thursday of the month); there's a walking tour leaflet you can use to see the entire neighborhood. A free trolley connects these downtown areas, or it's a short walk through lovely Murphy Park. Kitty-corner from the park is *The Bead Museum,* (623–931–2737; www.bead museumaz. org) a fascinating collection of beads from around the world, historic through recent. Beads come in all shapes and sizes and traditionally have been decorated with various techniques or simply left unadorned. Over the centuries they have been used for trade and currency, as amulets, and, of course, for jewelry and personal adornment. The museum is open Monday through Wednesday, Friday, and Saturday 10:00 A.M.–5:00 P.M.; Thursday 10:00 A.M.–8:00 P.M.; and Sunday 11:00 A.M.–4:00 P.M. Also in the trolley route or a fairly easy walk from Old Town is *Cerreta Candy Company,* (623–930–1000) at 5345 West Glendale Avenue, a family-operated chocolate factory where you can watch candy being made, buy gift assortments, and enjoy a sample or two.

On the opposite side of the Valley, *Tempe,* one of the oldest communities in the area, is known as the home of *Arizona State University* (ASU; 480–965–9011). The previously mentioned Grady Gammage Memorial Auditorium is definitely worth your time.

For a different kind of art work, wander into the ASU campus and head for the *Nelson Fine Arts Center* (480–965–2787; asuartmuseum. asu.edu). The 119,000-square-foot center, designed by Antoine Predock, is itself a work of art. The lavender-hued structures that make up the center are boldly geometric yet reflect the shapes you find in the Sonoran Desert. Inside, along with performing arts spaces, are 8,000 works of art in the ASU Art Museum, including an extensive collection of contemporary ceramics and Latin American folk and fine art.

ASU, incidentally, is where Jerry Lewis's character worked in his best-loved film, *The Nutty Professor;* you may recognize some of the buildings from the film on campus. *Sun Devil Stadium* is also the site of Super Bowl XXX. Tempe, however, doesn't need special events to draw a crowd. The whole downtown area is packed with college hangouts— pizza, Chinese food, coffeehouses, microbreweries—if you can't find something here that tempts your palate, you aren't really hungry.

The East Valley and Points South

*J*ust east of Tempe is *Mesa* (800–283–6372), another surprise in the Valley of the Sun. Recently graced with a face-lift, the downtown area is the site of *almost* everything you might want to see or do. The expanded *Mesa Southwest Museum* (480–644–2230) at 53 North Macdonald has the largest exhibition of animated, full-scale, "roaring" dinosaurs west of the Mississippi, plus an exhibit of sea life from the Jurassic and Paleozoic periods. A 50-foot waterfall, caves, and re-creations of Hohokam Indian dwellings are also part of the museum's exhibits. The museum is open Tuesday through Saturday 10:00 A.M.–5:00 P.M. and Sunday 1:00–5:00 P.M. Closed on holidays. Set among gardens, *The Arizona Temple Visitors Center* (480–964–7164) at 525 East Main Street is a well-known landmark in this city that was founded by the Mormons in 1878. Known for both its Easter Pageant (largest annual in the world) and its displays of twinkling lights during the holidays, the main attraction is its 10-foot Christus sculpture by Bertel Thorvaldsen.

Not far away are two museums that will be of special interest to aviation buffs or anyone with an interest in seeing preserved military aircraft of

World Wars I and II. Both the *Champlin Fighter Aircraft Museum* (480–830–4540) and *the Arizona Wing of the Confederate Air Force* (480–924–1940) are located adjacent to Falcon Field Airport near the crossroads of McKellips and Greenfield Roads. The Champlin features domestic and international aircraft of both wars as well as early jets. The Arizona Wing displays several of the greats of World War II, restored and maintained not just for display in Arizona but in flying condition and ready for takeoff to events around the country each year. Among their aircraft are the American B-17 *Sentimental Journey,* which is considered the most authentically restored of all the B-17s flying today; plus there is an example of a German Heinkel, and perhaps by the time you visit, a restored B-25 bomber of the type Jimmy Doolittle flew.

The Lower Salt River Recreation Area, which can be reached easily from Mesa, is a popular summer spot for "tubing" and river rafting trips. Weather permitting, the Salt is crammed with people on inner tubes, drifting lazily while their portable stereos compete for audio dominance. Others take guided tours of the river. Three companies not far from Mesa that provide equipment and transportation are *Salt River Recreation, Inc.* (480–984–3305), *Cimarron River Rafting Co.* (480–994–1199), and *Desert Voyagers Guided Raft Trips* (480–998–7238; www.desertvoyagers.com).

At the eastern end of the Valley of the Sun sits *Apache Junction,* located at the intersection of State Route 88 and U.S. 60. This town boasts several well-attended annual events. Ironically, given the town's name and very Southwestern heritage, one of the major yearly amusements is a *Renaissance Festival* (520–463–2700). Held weekends and holidays from mid-February through late March, this 30-acre re-creation of life in sixteenth-century England features performances by jugglers, musicians, dancers, and other entertainers. This merriment is intertwined with jousting matches and falconry demonstrations. There also are more than 200 vendors of food and crafts, and you can even see trained fleas perform. Incidentally, the "sister city" for this event is Sherwood Forest, England. Apache Junction celebrates its mining heritage in February with *Lost Dutchman Days.* Legend has it that sometime in the late 1880s Dutch miner Jacob Walz discovered a gold mine in the Superstition Mountains just outside of Apache Junction. The Superstitions, a 160,285-acre volcanic mountain range, is rocky and rugged throughout. When Walz died in 1891 without revealing the location of his mine, many treasure seekers flocked to the area to hunt for the Dutchman's riches. To this day no one has uncovered the location. Lost Dutchman Days events include a rodeo, a parade, and a carnival.

You can delve into the region's mining history any time of year by following the *Apache Trail,* a circular route into the *Tonto National Forest* that takes you to the *Goldfield Ghost Town,* a re-created 1890s mining town that features tours of a former mine, a scenic railroad, and includes the *Superstition Mountain Lost Dutchman Museum.* At the museum you can learn how prehistoric Indians lived in the area, see a model of the entire Superstition Mountain wilderness area, and study exhibits that tell you about natural history—rocks, ores, animals, and reptiles. One exhibit contains photos, furniture, and equipment from a family home; another displays equipment and clothing from the mounted troops that are part of Arizona history; and, perhaps most fun, there are twenty-three maps that show possible locations of the Lost Dutchman Mine. For tours contact Goldfield Ghost Town and Mine Tours (480–983–0333) at 4650 North Mammoth Mine Road. The route continues to Canyon Lake where you can ride the *Dolly Steamboat* through the inner waterways of the "Junior Grand Canyon" and learn more about plants and animals that live near the lake. Next stop, *Tortilla Flat, Arizona,* population six, where the combination restaurant, motel, saloon, gift shop, grocery store, and U.S. Post Office is a convenient place to stop for a "burger," chili, or an ice-cream cone.

I recommend that you contact a tour company if you'd like to get a close-up look at the Superstitions. Many hikers and prospectors have died because they didn't know the terrain well enough.

Traveling south from Apache Junction on U.S. 60 takes you to *Superior* (520–689–0200). Known by several names since the 1880s, the town was a mining center for about one hundred years. Lately Superior has earned a bit of a reputation as a movie set, serving as the setting for *The Prophecy,* a horror flick, and recently, Oliver Stone's *U-Turn.* Word has it that Stone selected the town because it retained a 1950s ambience, and set designers left behind many of the facades they created on the town's main street. Today visitors make the trek to Superior to tour the nearby *Boyce Thompson Arboretum* (520–689–2811). The arboretum contains more than 1,500 species of plants, as well as many birds and animals. Its specialties are desert and arid-land plants, including cacti and wildflowers of many colorful varieties. Created in 1924, it's the oldest and largest botanical garden in Arizona. There are more than six hiking trails throughout the grounds. Ranging from easy half-mile strolls to moderately rugged 3-mile hikes, these trails are especially popular in the fall and winter when the mild weather in this area encourages people to enjoy the great outdoors. In the vicinity is *Picket Post Mountain,* where in 1927 Colonel Boyce Thompson built a home into the stony face of a cliff. The house is now a museum, maintained just as Thompson, a copper magnate, left it. It's open 8:00 A.M.–5:00 P.M. daily. Dogs are permitted if leashed, and picnic tables are available.

Also nearby are the **Apache Tears Caves.** The caves contain many fine examples of black obsidian, known in the Southwest as "Apache tears." This dense, glassy volcanic rock is popular in many Southwestern jewelry designs. Visitors can chisel off an Apache tear for a small fee. The name Apache Tear comes from a heartbreaking legend. Just south of Superior is **Apache Leap** in Queen Creek Canyon. (You can reach this location by taking Highway 177 south from Superior and watching for the turnoff to Apache Leap.) On this site some 120 years ago, a cavalry detachment from Camp Pinal cornered seventy-five Apache warriors. Rather than submit to capture, they threw themselves off the cliff. Upon hearing of the warriors' fate, the women of the tribe cried tears that turned to stone. Despite the tragic history of this spot, today it's a good place to drive to for a get-away-from-it-all picnic lunch.

If your next destination is the Tucson area, take Route 177 south and you'll soon enter the tri-city area known as **SMOR** (San Manuel, Mammoth, Oracle Region). This area has a long history as a mining and ranching community, though today SMOR is better known for recreational offerings such as hiking, horseback riding, and bird-watching. North of Oracle on U.S. 89 is the **Tom Mix Monument,** a stone pillar topped by a metal silhouette of a riderless horse. This vaguely macabre statue commemorates the approximate spot where silent movie Western hero Tom Mix was killed when he drove his Cord automobile off the road. The horse (Tony, Mix's favorite mount) has been stolen from the monument several times over the years, so don't be too surprised if it seems to have moseyed off!

Also near the SMOR is the famous (or, depending upon your perspective, infamous) **Biosphere II** (800–828–2462; www.bio2.edu) on State Route 77. The Biosphere II was originally designed by a team of researchers put together by Texas billionaire Edward Bass to create a totally self-contained environment in the form of a giant, pyramid-shaped greenhouse that could be used to study how ecosystems work and also provide a prototype for civilizations of the future (i.e., on other planets). Plagued by personnel problems and dogged by allegations of cultism, the project, which planned to seal a group of researchers inside the facility for two years, became the butt of many jokes. Even the TV series *Cheers* made fun of the concept by putting character Lilith inside such a facility.

Biosphere II

In 1993 things came to a head when members of Biosphere II's scientific advisory board resigned, citing concerns over imprecise experiments. The following year, Bass, who reportedly had paid $150 million to build Biosphere II, stepped in and removed key members of the management team. Since then, the new management team, a subsidiary of Columbia University, has turned away from the concept of sealing crew members inside the five-story, 7.2-million-cubic-foot greenhouse. Instead they've concentrated on specific experiments dealing with assessing methods of irrigation, creating air-purification products that can be used in homes and commercial buildings, and pursuing other projects that produce tangible results. Today visitors can tour portions of the facility and see environments ranging from a tropical rain-forest to a coral reef. You can drop in at a Biosphere II laboratory and see actual experiments or shop in the gift shop and eat lunch or dinner in the restaurant. There also is a twenty-seven-suite hotel—the Inn at the Biosphere—in the neighborhood. Admission to the Biosphere is currently $12.95 for a guided tour. It's open from 10:00 A.M.–4:00 P.M. daily.

Nearby *Oracle* has a long history as a mining community. In fact in 1902 Buffalo Bill Cody staked out a gold claim in this area and for a while lived in a cabin above one of his mines. He squandered a large portion of his fortune on what was essentially a hoax (there was virtually no gold, and the tungsten ore he found was not enough for him to recoup his investment).

Like many Arizona towns Oracle has a dedicated group of artists of various disciplines and abilities. The artists range from potters to landscape painters to bronze sculptors. They host an annual weekend *Oracle Festival of Fine Art* (520–896–9200), usually in March. During the festival there are tours of the artists' studios, art discussions, and performing arts events. Year-round, Oracle has a number of galleries and shops that display local artists. For information on the SMOR area, contact San

Manuel/Mammoth/Oracle Chamber of Commerce (520–896–9322), P.O. Box 1886, Oracle, AZ 85623.

Another off-the-beaten-path route to Tucson is through *Florence*, home to *Pinal County Historical Museum* (520–868–4382) and the McFarland Historical State Park. Florence is also a stone's throw away from such attractions as a group of petroglyphs and coke ovens off Kelvin Road, which is off a four-wheel-drive trail over private property. Check with Greater Florence Chamber of Commerce (520–868–9433 or 800–437–9433; www.info@florence.az.org), P.O. Box 929, Florence, AZ 85232. In town the visitors center is at 291 Bailey Street, in the historic district.

The *McFarland Historical State Park* (520–868–5216), on the corner of Main and Ruggles in Florence, was named after Ernest W. McFarland, the only American known to have served his state as an elected official in all three branches of government. It's the site of the *first Pinal County Courthouse,* an adobe block building constructed in 1878 that housed prisoners and provided offices for lawmen until 1891, when a larger facility was constructed. It was quite a hellhole in the early days. Before improvements to the building in 1882, the jail was a windowless adobe cubicle with one entrance that was covered by burlap. Prisoners were chained to a boulder buried in the center of the jail. Visitors can see the improved 1882 jail, the sheriff's office, and the court recorder's office. A nearby archive houses exhibits related to the governmental career of Ernest McFarland. McFarland State Park is open for self-guided tours Thursday through Monday from 8:00 A.M. to 5:00 P.M.

The *second Pinal County Courthouse,* built in 1891, still exists as well. Located on Pinal between 11th and 13th Streets, it is a large, rather ornate red brick building with a clock tower. Incidentally, this is the courthouse where Pearl Hart, the last known stagecoach robber in the United States, was tried in 1899 and sentenced to five years in the Territorial Prison at Yuma. Guided walking tours of Florence's historic downtown district can be arranged by calling (520) 868–5216.

If you'd like to hang around Florence for a while, check into the *Inn at Rancho Sonora* (520–868–8000) at 9198 North Highway 79, a 1930s adobe guest ranch. The rooms have been renovated and redecorated in Western fashion, but with the modern comfort conveniences of dual-paned windows and air conditioning. The inn also has a pool and a hot tub. Rates start at $59.

From Florence you can take Highway 287 west and Highway 87 south to the *Casa Grande National Monument.* Casa Grande was a Hohokam settlement built around A.D. 1150. Theories abound, including everything from family dwelling to astronomical observatory, regarding the purpose for the large adobe structure that still stands here in the midst of the desert. It's one of the best-preserved sites of its kind in the state. Stop by the visitors center to get a brochure and take the self-guided tour. If you have the time, stay for one of the informative talks given by a park ranger on the history of the Casa Grande ruins.

The major annual event for this area is the *O'Odham Tash,* a celebration of Native American culture usually held in February. Festivities are open to the general public. You'll hear traditional music of several varieties, including Waila, a kind of rock-and-roll polka. Watch colorful ceremonial dancers compete for awards and browse through arts and crafts, including baskets, rugs, paintings, and jewelry. You can also sample O'Odham cuisine. An all-Indian rodeo rounds out the events. Call the Casa Grande Chamber of Commerce at (800) 916–1515 or log onto www.casagrandechamber.org for more information.

Continuing on Highway 87 south takes you past farming communities that sprout forth like an emerald beard across the stubbly face of the desert. Highway 87 merges into I–10 a few miles south of the tiny town of Picacho. Just east of the town is *Picacho Peak* (520–466–3183; www.pr.state.az.us), a craggy, saguaro-dotted mountain that in the spring is covered with wildflowers. This is the site of the Battle of Picacho Pass, Arizona's only Civil War battle (military purists insist it was only a skirmish).

In any case, the military engagement took place on April 15, 1862, when Union troops commanded by Lt. James Barrett fired upon Confederates led by Lt. Jack Swilling. This is the same Jack Swilling who later was instrumental in digging Phoenix's irrigation canals. On the day of the Battle of Picacho Pass, however, he was intent only on pursuing victory for the Southern cause. In the ensuing action, Barrett and two Union privates were killed. Fearing that more Union troops were on the way, Swilling's forces retreated. That was a wise move because within a few days the Union army marched through Picacho Pass on the way to Tucson. Each spring (usually March), reenactors stage this battle as well as scenes of frontier life. Picacho Peak is a state park, with facilities including rest rooms, picnic areas, campgrounds, and an easy to moderately difficult nature trail.

PLACES TO STAY IN CENTRAL ARIZONA

PHOENIX
Hyatt Regency Phoenix,
122 North 2nd Street,
85004;
(602) 252–1234 or
(800) 233–1234.
Right downtown across
from the Civic Plaza with
712 rooms and suites.
Rooftop revolving restaurant for great view of the
entire Valley of the Sun.

GLENDALE
Best Western
Phoenix/Glendale,
5940 North West Grand
Avenue, 85301;
(623) 939 9431 or
(800) 333–7172.
Near Old Town Glendale
and Catlin Court.

MESA
Sheraton Mesa Hotel and
Convention Center,
200 North Centennial Way,
85201;
(480) 898–8300 or
(800) 456–MESA.
Not far from downtown
with 273 spacious, newly
decorated rooms.

SCOTTSDALE
Old Town Scottsdale Hotel
and Conference Center,
7353 East Indian School
Road, 85251;
(480) 994–9203 or
(800) 695–6995.
Near the art galleries and
shops of the Old Town
district.

TEMPE
Red Roof Inn,
1701 West Baseline Road,
85283; (480) 413–1188 or
(800) 633–8300.
Right off I–10, near
Peterson House Museum
and not too far from downtown Tempe.

PLACES TO EAT IN CENTRAL ARIZONA

GLENDALE
Haus Murphy's,
5819 West Glendale
Avenue, 85301;
(623) 939–2480.
German food on the main
street of Old Town Glendale.

MESA
Mango's,
44 West Main Street, 85201;
(480) 464–5700.
Another Mexican possibility in the heart of downtown shopping not far
from Mesa Southwest
Museum.

SCOTTSDALE
5 & Diner,
9069 East Indian Bend
Road, 85250;
(480) 949–1957.
In Scottsdale Pavilions
Mall off Pima Road. Fifties
diner with jukeboxes playing the oldies. Breakfasts,
burgers, and blue-plate
specials.

Web Sites for Central Arizona

Arizona Office of Tourism's Web site,
www.arizonaguide.com,
has links to Web sites for the following cities:

Carefree/Cave Creek, Chandler, Florence, Fountain Hills,
Glendale, Mesa, Peoria, Phoenix, Scottsdale, and Tempe.

Southern Arizona

The Southwestern Corner

Yuma (928–783–0071 or 800–293–0071), on I-8, exists among several worlds: It's only a few minute's drive from either the California state line or the Mexican border. It's also in the midst of a desert area, yet it's bordered by the Colorado River and has more than 150,000 acres dedicated to agriculture.

Despite its dichotomies, *Yuma* has a long, colorful history as a distinctive part of Arizona. It was originally named Colorado City (after the river) and then Arizona City, finally taking the name of the Native American tribe that had long called the area home. Puns were inevitable, and a few years back the suggestion was made that the town adopt the slogan "You'll Love Our Sense of Yuma."

In the nineteenth century the town was a crossing point for the famous Mormon Battalion as well as Kit Carson and California gold seekers. In the 1850s the invention of the shallow-draft steamboat made Yuma a major stop on the Colorado River for boats taking supplies to army posts or mining camps. Its territorial prison, built in 1875, housed some of the West's most notorious desperados, and in modern times the town has become not only an important agricultural center (labor organizer Cesar Chavez grew up here) but also the site for a Marine Corps Air Station and an Army Proving Ground.

For history buffs, Yuma has a number of interesting museums. The *Yuma Crossing State Historic Park* (928–329–0471; www.pr.state.az.us) at Fourth Avenue located beyond the railroad tracks along the river behind City Hall, was a vital distribution point for military equipment 130 years ago. Several original buildings, including the quartermaster's office and the commanding officer's quarters, have been restored. The depot is operated as a living history museum, complete with authentically costumed guides. It's open daily during the winter months; from May 1 through October 31, it's open Thursday through Monday.

SOUTHERN ARIZONA

AUTHOR'S TOP PICKS

Arizona-Sonora Desert Museum

Kitt Peak National Observatory

Tanque Verde Guest Ranch

Mission San Xavier del Bac

Tubac

San Pedro and Southwestern Railway

Ramsey Canyon Preserve

Bisbee shops and galleries

Chiricahua Mountains

Club Congress

Sabino Canyon

The Yuma Territorial Prison State Park (928–783–4771; www.pr.state.az.us/parkhtml/yuma.html) at 100 Prison Hill Road at the east end of First Avenue is another popular attraction. No film about the Old West is complete without at least one reference to this infamous Iron Bar Hotel. Historians argue over whether the prison, built in 1876, was actually a "hellhole," as it's often depicted. Certainly inmates would have found it cramped, dark, and hot. Yet it had one of the first libraries in the state, electric fans, and many prison sentences were brief. There are video presentations on the history of the prison at 11:00 A.M., 2:00 P.M., and 3:30 P.M. Visit the prison on the second or fourth Sunday of the month, and you can watch Old West shoot-outs staged by the Yuma Vigilantes.

One of the strangest bits of history in the area is the *McPhail Bridge,* 18 miles north of Yuma on Highway 95. The bridge, sometimes referred to locally as the "bridge to nowhere," was built in 1929 as a route across the Gila River. When the Gila was rerouted for agricultural projects, the bridge was left stranded, straddling only desert. The structure, which resembled a scaled-down version of the Golden Gate bridge, is named

Sand Dune Stand-ins

*A*rizona's deserts are among the world's most verdant, so visitors looking for a Sahara-like landscape will find more vegetation than bargained for. However, a sandier setting exists west of Yuma. Travel west on I–8 to Gray's Well exit and follow the frontage road. You'll wind up surrounded by sand dunes that have served as stand-ins for Middle Eastern dunes in many TV shows and films, dating back to about 1921 when Valentino's The Sheik was filmed here. All three versions of Beau Geste were at least partially lensed in these dunes, as well as the Jimmy Stewart movie The Flight of the Phoenix. (At the very end of the film, a patched-together plane heads over these dunes and disappears from sight. In real life it crashed just out of camera range, killing the pilot.) The tremendously popular George Lucas film Star Wars was partially filmed here, as was the science fiction hit Stargate. There are no real markers or landmarks here to photograph—just miles of sand—so bring your imagination and maybe a few props like a light saber or your pet Ewok.

Top Annual Events in Southern Arizona

January

Willcox: Wings over Willcox. *Sandhill Crane Celebration, guided tours, includes a "hawk stalk," seminars, workshops, field trips, bird-watching (520–384–2272 or 800–200–2272). Third weekend in January.*

February

Tucson: Arizona Mineral and Fossil Show *(303–674–2713).*

Benson: Territorial Days. *Crafts, auto show, music, dances, games, reenactments, auction, exhibits, contests, balloon festival (520–586–9706 or 520–586–2842).*

Sierra Vista: Cochise Cowboy Poetry and Music Gathering. *Storytellers, reciters, singers and musicians, artists with national recognition. (520–459–3868 or 800–288–3861). First weekend in February.*

Tubac: Festival of the Arts. *Juried artists, entertainment, and demonstrations (520–398–2704).*

Tucson: Arizona State Museum's Southwest Indian Art Fair *(520–621–6302).*

Tucson: La Fiesta de los Vaqueros. *More than seventy years old, this PRCA rodeo is America's largest, outdoor, midwinter rodeo (520–741–2233 or 800–964–5662).*

Yuma: Jaycees Silver Spur Rodeo Parade. *For more than fifty years, the largest in Yuma (928–344–5451).*

March

Ajo: O'odham Day Celebration *(520–387–6849).*

Tombstone: Territorial Days. *Arizona fire cart championship races, all-pet parade (520–457–9317 or 888–457–3929).*

April

Bisbee: La Vuelta de Bisbee. *Top amateur men and women cyclists from throughout the United States and abroad wind up and down the roads of historic Old Bisbee (520–432–5421; anhop@primenet.com; www.azcycling.com).*

Tucson: Bank One International Mariachi Conference. *Educational workshop, concerts, mariachi showcase, art exhibit, Garibaldi Fiesta, golf tournament (520–884–9920).*

May

Sierra Vista: The Festival of the Southwest. *Food, live entertainment, crafts, and art (520–417–6980 or 520–458–6940).*

Tombstone: Wyatt Earp Days. *Gunfights, public hanging, saloon girls, fashion show, parade, dancing, live country/western band (520–457–3291).*

Tucson: Cinco de Mayo. *Artists, music, folklorico dancers, commemorating Mexico's victory against the French at Puebla (520–292–9326).*

August

Sierra Vista: Southwest Wings Birding Festival. *Field trips, displays, lectures, bat stalks, owl prowls, displays, arts, and crafts (520–432–5421).*

Tombstone: Vigilante Day. *Shoot-outs, hangings, concert, chili cook-off, saloon girls (520–457–3197).*

September

Bisbee: Brewery Gulch Days. *Horseshoe and waterball tournament, kiddie carnival, live music, dunk tank, pet parade, Miz Ol' Biz contest, mining games, cake walk (520–432–5578 or 520–432–5421).*

Tombstone: Rendezvous of Gunfighters. *Shows in the O.K. Corral by the best western groups from around the United States (520–457–3197).*

October

Benson: Butterfield Overland Stage Days. *Celebration of overland mail route from St. Louis to San Francisco, reenactments, stage rides, arts and crafts, entertainment, dances, car show (520–586–2842).*

Bisbee: Gem and Mineral Show. *Dealers, display of rare minerals, outdoor show, field trips (520–432–5421 or 520–432–3142).*

Bisbee: Fiber Arts Festival. *Fashion show, fiber animals such as sheep and llamas, displays, demonstrations, workshops, guest speakers (520–432–5421).*

Bisbee: Bisbee 1000—The Great Stairclimb *(520–432–5421).*

Patagonia: Fall Festival. *Juried arts and crafts, country western, bluegrass, folk, mariachi, Latin jazz, rock & roll, Saturday night dance, western events (520–394–0060 or 888–794–0060). Second weekend in October.*

Sierra Vista: Festival of Color. *Annual hot-air balloon rally (520–458–6940).*

Tombstone: Helldorado Days. *Oldest celebration, with shoot-outs, fashion show, and street entertainment (520–457–2550). Third weekend in October.*

Tucson: La Fiesta de los Chiles. *International cuisine, entertainment, music, artisans and crafts people (520–326–9686).*

Willcox: Rex Allen Days. *Celebration of singing cowboy star Rex Allen (520 384 2272 or 800–200–2272). First weekend in October.*

November

Bisbee: Festival of Lights. *Live nativity in historic Bisbee (520–432–5446).*

Bisbee: Historic Home Tour *(520–432–5421 or 520–432–5446).*

Tombstone: Emmett Kelly Jr. Days. *Clown contests, clown roundup, clown costume contest, performances, street dance (520–457–9213 or 520–457–9397).*

Tucson: Western Music Festival. *Concerts, workshops, jam sessions by western musicians, western merchandise, western art (520–743–9794).*

Yuma: Colorado River Crossing Balloon Festival. *Sunrise balloon liftoffs, sunset balloon glow and fireworks, entertainment (928–539–2022).*

December

Tucson: Luminaria Nights. *Holiday lights, music by local groups and choirs (520–326–9686).*

Tucson: Fourth Avenue Street Fair. *Arts and crafters, community stage, entertainers, and "Kidstreat" (520–624–5004 or 800–933–2477).*

after Harry McPhail, a former territorial prison guard who ventured into the mining industry and once had claims in this area.

See Yuma County by train by boarding the **Yuma Valley Railroad** (928–783–3456) at the end of Madison Avenue. A diesel engine pulls a restored Pullman Coach along the banks of the Colorado while a historian/guide tells passengers about the area. The railroad operates from October through June.

A more leisurely method of seeing the western edge of Yuma is aboard a paddleboat. *The* **Colorado King I** *Paddleboat* (928–782–2412) is a replica of the craft that used to cruise the Colorado River in Mark Twain's time. Dining tours are available. The paddleboat tours operate October through June. You can also see the river on a small cruiser with a group. **Yuma River Tours** (928–783–4400) offers day trips, including lunch.

Numerous restaurant chains populate Yuma, but so do longtime family-operated businesses. One of these is **Lute's Casino** (928–782–2192) at 221 Main Street. Lute's offers sandwiches and other fast-food items in a somewhat wacky atmosphere.

Many national chains are on standby to house road warriors visiting Yuma. Among the top choices are **Coronado Motel** (928–783–4453) at 233 4th Avenue, which offers rooms with a refrigerator and microwave. The **Best Western Inn Suites Hotel** (928–783–8341) at 1450 Castle Dome Avenue features complimentary continental breakfast. Nearby the **Shilo Inn Resort Hotel** (928–782–9511) at 1550 South Castle Dome Avenue has a free buffet breakfast.

Head east on I–8 to **Gila Bend** (928–683–2002). The town got its name from the sharp bend in the Gila River that used to occur at this point before the river was diverted for agricultural purposes.

Today visitors to Gila Bend can step back into history in a variety of ways. Just west of town is petroglyph-covered **Painted Rocks** (928–780–8090). You can reach this wildlife area by taking I–8 to exit 102. The exact meaning of these 1,000-year-old Hohokam etchings is unknown. People, reptiles, and geometric doodles cover the black basalt rocks. There's a recreational lake and a picnic area here, so if you have the time, pack a lunch, bring a sketch pad, and try to decode all the combinations of the primitive alphabet depicted on Painted Rocks. The *Agua Caliente Hotel and Hot Springs* ruins are also located just west of town. To reach them, exit from I–8 onto Sentinel and follow the road. The former hotel and surrounding adobe buildings—constructed to take advantage of the area's status as a stage stop as well as the supposed therapeutic values of the water—are still partially standing. You can pose by a crumbling adobe wall and then send copies of the picture to your friends and family. Tell them you've picked out your retirement home. You won't be able to relax in the hot springs, however; they dried up years ago.

In downtown Gila Bend is the *Gila Bend Historical Museum* (928–683–2002) at 644 West Pima Street. Dedicated to the preservation of archaeological and historical finds, it includes information gathered from the Hohokam Ceremonial Platform that's near town. The platform dates from A.D. 800; currently there are plans to re-excavate and open up some of the area as a state park. The museum is open daily from 8:00 A.M. to 4:00 P.M.; admission is free. The museum is also the visitors information center.

Gila Bend is home to several unusual dwellings. The former *Stout Hotel,* at the corner of Pima and Capitol Streets, is a poured concrete

The Oatman Massacre

*S*outh of the hotel ruins on Sentinel is the site of the **Oatman Massacre.** A large, white cross on a nearby plateau stands as a monument to the Oatman family. On March 19, 1851, Royce and Mary Ann Oatman and their seven children were part of a Mormon pilgrimage to the Arizona/ California border area. They were camped on this spot when a group of Yavapai Indians approached and asked for food and tobacco. Royce complied but, fearful that he wouldn't have enough for his family, refused the Yavapais' request for seconds. The family, with the exception of fifteen-year-old Lorenzo, fourteen-year-old Olive, and her younger sister Mary Ann, was brutally slain. Lorenzo survived by playing dead, while the two girls were taken as captives. Mary Ann died soon after, and Olive was sold to the Mohave Indians and later ransomed back into white society (in a bizarre twist, she became a celebrity as a result of her ordeal, though her story was largely used as anti–Native American propaganda). The actual site of the killings is just east of the roadway, but it can only be reached by a four-wheel-drive vehicle.

building constructed around 1929 as a first-rate hotel for railroad and automobile travelers. It had air conditioning and steam heat and an ice plant in the basement. In its heyday its many famous guests included Clark Gable and Carole Lombard. Incidentally, the pair appears to have been quite fond of Arizona, having been on the guest lists of several other hotels statewide, including the Monte Vista in Flagstaff and Phoenix's San Carlos Hotel and Arizona Biltmore Resort. Now part of the hotel is being used as a general store. The rest is awaiting restoration, but no date has been set to begin yet.

Across an *arroyo* (a streambed to non-Southwesterners), just west of the town's ice plant, is a curious-looking structure built of railroad ties. Constructed in the midst of the Great Depression by **Harvey Brown** (aka "Jungle Jim" because of the pith helmet he wore), this once was a store that sold everything from sandwiches to luggage. Brown's customers were vagrants like himself, and, ironically, recent reports are that the building—whose exact ownership is in question—is now being used by squatters. If you're interested in twentieth-century U.S. history, this unusual building is worth a visit because it represents a typical American's boot-strap response to hard times.

Only a handful of restaurants operate in Gila Bend. A safe bet is a stop at one of the fast-food eateries that beckon hungry travelers or the twenty-four-hour coffee shop at the **Best Western Space Age Lodge** (928–683–2273) at 401 East Pima. Whether you're hungry or not, you have to stop by the kitschy roadside inn. This priceless piece of Americana was built in the early 1960s and for years had a Sputnik-style satellite attached to the roof. It was recently remodeled, and a brand new spacecraft now sits atop the roof.

Less than an hour south of Gila Bend on Highway 85 is the tiny town of **Ajo** (520–387–7742). Though the word ajo (*ahh-ho*) is Spanish for garlic and also is used as a mild expletive, some historians believe the town's name actually originated from a similar-sounding Tohono O'Odham word for paint (ore from this area was used for making pigment). In any case Ajo was the oldest-known mine site in the state, and until the 1980s Phelps Dodge ran a sizable copper-mining operation out of here. The mines originally were made profitable during World War I by John C. Greenway, who also gets the credit for building the town's palm tree–shaded **Spanish Colonial Plaza** in Ajo's center. The plaza is a traditional town square created in a Spanish Colonial revival style. In the midst of the plaza is a large, green park and surrounding it are shops, restaurants, and two churches. To the south of the plaza is a Federated church built in 1926. Just north of that structure sits a mission-style Catholic church constructed in 1924.

A number of buildings from the 1920s and before are still standing. *Curley School,* southwest of the plaza on Vanand, was constructed in 1919. The *Train Depot,* directly northeast of the plaza, dates from 1915. *New Cornelia Hotel,* just east of Curley School, was constructed in 1916. Plans are in the works to restore it as a restaurant. The exteriors of these buildings, most done in Spanish Colonial revival, are easily incorporated into a walking tour. Stop by the Ajo Chamber of Commerce on Highway 85 just south of the Plaza and ask for a self-guided tour map.

A building that has been restored is now a charming bed-and-breakfast inn. The *Guest House Inn* (520–387–6133) at 700 Guest House Road is a sort of Southwestern plantation house, built in 1925 by the Greenways as a guest house for their visitors. The inn offers four rooms with private baths. The rooms are furnished in Southwestern style, some with Victorian antiques. Breakfast is hearty, and from the patio you can watch a variety of native birds, including quail and cactus wrens.

Ajo today is one part retirement community, one part snowbird haven, and one part bedroom community for people who don't mind the two-hour commute to Phoenix or Tucson.

Ajo's gorgeous mountain views and charming Old World architecture are certainly enchanting. For some, however, Ajo is merely a stopping-off point on the way to *Organ Pipe Cactus National Monument* (520–387–6849; www.nps.gov/orpi), located south off Highway 85. If you were to take a giant octopus, turn it upside down, and plant it in the dirt, you would have a rough idea of what an organ pipe cactus looks like. In color and form these cacti resemble saguaros, but unlike saguaros, they have a half-dozen or more long arms reaching out from a center point. They are quite spectacular, especially during a spring bloom. This fantastic show typically occurs mid-March through mid-April.

The monument, by the way, is the starting point for notorious *El Camino del Diablo*—"the Devil's Highway." Over the years this stretch of godforsaken road has claimed numerous lives (more than 400 during the California gold rush). If you've got a four-wheel-drive vehicle, you may want to attempt this hot, bumpy, desolate trek that ends near Yuma. Because there are no road services along the way, plan on taking plenty of supplies (especially water) for you and your car. A safer, easier drive over a graded dirt road can be taken from near the Organ Pipe National Monument Visitor Center. Called the *Ajo Mountain Drive,* this 21-mile loop will take you through the Diablo Mountain Range to Mount Ajo and back to the visitors center. Along the way you'll see many varieties of cacti and desert creatures. In early spring you may see wildflowers, and in April or May cactus blossoms dot the landscape.

After the monument take State 86 east toward Tucson. Just past the town of Sells, turn south onto Highway 386. This route will lead you 6,900 feet above sea level to the top of Kitt Peak in the Quinlan Mountains. The view, which takes in the neighboring Baboquivari Mountains and long stretches of Sonoran desert, is not only quite spectacular, but this is the site of *NOAO Kitt Peak National Observatory* (520–318–8726), the world's largest. Though the climb up a paved road to the observatory is a bit steep, if you're interested in astronomy, it's worth the effort. The observatory's McMath solar telescope is the largest aperture solar telescope in the world. The visitors center gives one-hour-long guided tours of either the 4-meter or the 2.1-meter telescope as well as the solar telescope. Picnic grounds with barbecue grills also share space on the peak, and many tourists to Kitt Peak bring lunch. The observatory is located at 950 North Cherry, Tucson, and is open daily 9:00 A.M.–4:00 P.M.

Downtown and East Tucson

From Kitt Peak, *Tucson* (800–638–8350) is the next major stop. Known as the Old Pueblo by locals, Tucson was founded in 1775 and is one of the oldest continually inhabited sites in the United States. Archeologists have discovered Hohokam artifacts that date back thousands of years. The community is an eclectic meld of Native American, Mexican, Spanish, Asian, and European cultures. Consider the fact that the town was founded on the site of an ancient Indian settlement by an Irishman serving in the Spanish Army!

Trivia
Tucson has more than 150 Mexican restaurants.

You can reach Tucson from Kitt Peak by taking Highway 86 east. Once you reach the Tucson city limits, Highway 86 turns into Ajo Way. This puts you on the southwest side of the city. Take the I–10 west freeway entrance from Ajo Way, and follow I–10 to the Broadway Boulevard exit. As you exit onto Broadway, you'll be driving into downtown Tucson.

While you're cruising on I–10, you'll notice that Tucson is surrounded by mountains. To the west are the Tucson Mountains; to the east, the Rincons. Directly north are the Santa Catalinas, and down south are the Santa Ritas. Some of the peaks are snow-capped in winter, and *Mount Lemmon*

Trivia

Dueling deities: The city of Douglas's Church Square is believed to be the only place in the world with four churches on four corners in the same block.

in the Catalinas is known for being the southernmost skiable peak in the United States. The community of **Summerhaven** near the top of the mountain is a cool summer getaway only an hour's drive from the city. Gift shops, a general store, and rental cabins line the short main street. If you're interested in staying on Mount Lemmon, try *Mt. Lemmon Cabins and Cookies* (520–576–1542). The proprietors rent five small but cozy cabin suites and bake goodies, such as chocolate chip cookies, to sell to the public. Farther up the mountain, *Ski Valley* offers a full season of snow sports. In the off-season the ski lift still runs, providing visitors with great views of the Catalinas.

You can reach Mount Lemmon by taking I–10 north to Grant Road. Follow Grant Road until it reaches the far east side of Tucson. The road will become Tanque Verde. Stay on Tanque Verde until you reach the Catalina Highway. Turn left onto the Catalina Highway and drive north. The road will take you all the way up Mount Lemmon.

Mountains are very important to Tucsonans. For one thing, they provide landmarks. While you're traveling anywhere on the northwest side of Tucson, glance to the west and you'll notice a small peak with an "A" whitewashed onto the rocks. *Sentinel Peak* ("A" Mountain to locals) is where the community called *Chukson* ("spring at the foot of the black mountain") began. The "A"—whitewashed every year by University of Arizona freshmen—has been a prominent monument since 1914. There is a narrow, paved road that takes you all the way up Sentinel Peak. The view of the city from the peak, especially as the sun sets and lights begin to twinkle on, is quite spectacular. To reach Sentinel Peak take the Congress Street exit from I–10 and head west toward the peak. One note of caution: You probably don't want to linger on the peak after dark; Sentinel Peak at night becomes a favorite "parking" and hangout spot for high schoolers and others.

From Sentinel Peak you can reach the downtown by simply driving east on Congress Street. Less than two decades ago, downtown Tucson was dead: mortally wounded by new, centrally located shopping malls that forced the downtown department stores to close up. Downtown— roughly bounded by 4th Avenue on the east, Church Street on the west, Council on the south, and 12th Street on the north—became a graveyard that no one wanted to whistle past after dark.

Today the once-silent area, together with neighboring districts such as the university area, is as vibrant and exciting as a jazz sax solo. The

The sun shines 350 days a year in Tucson.

backbeat of the new downtown comes from the *Tucson Arts District,* which regularly holds *Downtown Nights.* During these events the cafes, art galleries, and boutique shops that line both sides of Congress Street, Broadway Boulevard, and other downtown routes stay open late. Street musicians play in the square, and you'll see everything from strolling Shakespearean actors to aging hippies selling tie-dyed T-shirts. For example, members of the Tucson Symphony Orchestra sometimes play short concerts aimed at getting kids interested in music. Seasonal *Art Walks* are another project aimed at getting locals and tourists into the downtown area. You don't have to wait for a special day, however, to enjoy the galleries, performance venues, and cafes. The following paragraphs direct you to some of the area's most unique and interesting attractions.

Dinnerware Gallery (520–792–4503; www.dinnerwarearts.com) at 135 East Congress always has interesting exhibits. One month the gallery might pair a sculptor who creates realistic images of people with an installation by a performance artist who will display a dining room set wrapped in newspaper. You'll discover as you visit these and the other downtown galleries that art in Tucson is very diverse. Some of it is heavily influenced by the Southwest. Much of it, however, is cosmopolitan. You'll see abstract and impressionist and pop art that would look right at home in a New York high-rise apartment as well as pieces that portray coyotes, Native Americans, Spanish missions, and other classic symbols of Tucson's history.

Within walking distance of the downtown galleries is the newly renovated and expanded *Tucson Museum of Art and Historic Block* (520–624–2333; www.tucsonarts.com) at 140 North Main Street. The museum, considered to be a mini-Guggenheim in its interior design, houses numerous permanent collections, including a large exhibit of pre-Columbian art. The courtyard in front of the museum is often used for events, including blues and jazz concerts as well as block-party–style fund-raisers for the museum.

Across the courtyard from the TMA is the historic *Stevens/Duffield House* (La Casa Córdova) at 150 North Main Avenue.

On the *Presidio* square are other historic houses—the *Romero House* from the 1860s, the *Corbett House* built in 1907, and *La Casa Cordova* built in the pre– and post–Civil War years. The *Fish House* (aka Goodman Pavilion) built in 1867 now houses a collection of Western art.

Tucson has truly emerged as a hot spot for haute cuisine. Great choices include **Barrio Bar & Grill** (520–629–0191) at 135 South 6th Avenue, a downtown bistro, and **Scordato's** at 4405 West Speedway Boulevard, which features a bistro-style atmosphere with light Italian cuisine.

Mount Lemmon, in the Santa Catalina Mountains north of Tucson, is the southernmost ski area in the continental United States and is the only mountain in the country named after the first woman who climbed it— Sarah Lemmon.

As you might suspect of a town located smack-dab in the heart of Old West territory, quite a few rough-and-tumble incidents took place in the downtown area. At the corner of Church and Pennington Streets, a couple of blocks south of North Main Avenue, a bizarre shooting involving two prominent members of the community occurred in 1891. C. Handy, the chief surgeon for the Southern Pacific Railroad (and one-time chancellor for the nascent University of Arizona) shot and killed Francis J. Heney, the lawyer representing Handy's wife in their divorce.

A few blocks farther south on Main Avenue and Simpson beyond the Convention Center, in the neighborhood known as **Barrio Historico,** stands an adobe wall with a plaque dedicated to **El Tiradito** ("the little castaway"). The story goes that many years ago, a young sheepherder who lived with his wife and his in-laws on a ranch outside of town fell in love with his wife's mother. While meeting in town for an adulterous liaison, they were caught by the sheepherder's father-in-law, who killed the young man and buried him. Because the sheepherder was buried in unconsecrated ground, he was forever doomed as a sinner—a castaway. Today, locals light candles and leave hand-printed prayers at this wishing shrine.

Next to El Tiradito is **El Minuto Cafe** (520–882–4145) at 354 South Main. It's a very popular Mexican restaurant featuring authentic versions of Sonoran cuisine. During weekdays it's difficult to get a table at lunch. It's equally busy in the evening if there's an event at the nearby Tucson Convention Center or the Arizona Theatre Company Temple of Music and Art.

A brief jog to the north is **Old Town Artisans** (www.oldtownartisans.com) at 201 North Court Avenue. It's a collection of fine art, jewelry, and crafts shops that sits in the area of the original Spanish presidio. Two front rooms contain adobe blocks dating back to the 1860s. The complex also includes **La Cocina** (520–622–0351), with indoor and outdoor dining, a restaurant also known as **Two Micks Cantina Grill.**

On Congress Avenue there's lots to see and do. You might want to peruse the many antiques and secondhand shops. At the end of the street is the historic **Hotel Congress** at 311 East Congress. A funky sort of place, the hotel provides basic accommodations and houses the **Club Congress,** which features live music on weekends (i.e. current alternative). The **Cup Cafe,** where you can get gourmet coffee and a bite to eat, is also within the hotel complex. The club and cafe are considered the "be-seen" hot spots in downtown Tucson.

At 330 South Scott Avenue is the **Arizona Theatre Company Temple of Music and Art** (520–622–2823; www.arizonatheater.org), a beautiful complex that includes a cabaret theater, a main auditorium, a cafe, and an art gallery. Performances by the Arizona Theatre Company are held here, as are concerts and other cultural events. The Arizona Theatre Company's season is usually September through May. Tickets may be purchased online.

About a three-minute drive east of downtown is **4th Avenue** (Merchant's Association; 520–624–5004), a lively strip of real estate that has the atmosphere (and the history) of San Francisco's Haight-Ashbury neighborhood. In the 1960s and 1970s, the businesses in this sleepy residential area were dominated by head shops and smoky bars where (nearly) free love and illegal drugs flowed. Today 4th Avenue has really cleaned up its act. The eclectic mix of shops includes **Bisonwitches Bar and Deli** (520–740–1541), a restaurant and bar; **Native Seed Search** (520–622–5561); **Maloneys** (520–388–9355); and **Above and Below the Equator** (520–792– 4647), a diverse gallery featuring sculptures, paintings, musical instruments, and other treasures from around the world. Award-winning designer Dee Williams also sells some of her jewelry here. Other shops specialize in antique clothing, such as **How Sweet It Was** (520–623–9845) at 531 North 4th Avenue and **Desert Vintage & Costume** (520–620–1570) at 636 North 4th Avenue.

Lots of restaurants to choose from guarantee that you won't go hungry. **Caruso's** (520–624–5765) at 434 North 4th Avenue has been serving Italian food to Tucsonans for about fifty years. Across the street, **Delectables** (520–884–9289) at 533 North 4th Avenue offers a variety of gourmet items, including fruit and cheese plates. If your sweet tooth gets the better of you, stop at the corner of 6th Street and 4th Avenue to find the **Chocolate Iguana** (520–798–1211) at 500 North 4th Avenue. It sells all sorts of candy, baked goods, and coffee drinks. It also has an interesting selection of greeting cards.

Fourth Avenue is best known locally for its two annual weekend street fairs—one usually runs in early December, and one is in late March or early April. Besides arts, crafts, and food booths (where you can sample some wonderful Tohono O'Odham frybread), the fairs feature street entertainers and representatives from all sorts of worthy human rights/animal rights groups. During a typical street fair, 4th Avenue is blocked off between University Boulevard and 9th Street, and exhibitors' booths are set up down the center of the avenue. Additionally, the sidewalks are taken over by people doing face painting and hair weaving and musicians playing everything from folk standards to doo-wop ballads. These events are extremely popular and draw Tucsonans of every background and visitors from every state. Expect to park at least four or five blocks away from 4th Avenue—and to part with a few bucks for a spot. The fairs usually start Friday afternoon.

To leave 4th Avenue you can simply drive out of the neighborhood via University Boulevard, or you can take the trolley. The *Old Pueblo Trolley* (520–792–1802), reinstalled just a few years ago (it originally ran from 1906 to 1930), takes riders down University past shops and restaurants to the main gate of the University of Arizona. On Tucson's fairly flat urban streets, it isn't quite the hair-raising, white-knuckle trip that San Francisco's streetcars take up Powell Street, but it is a lot of fun. The all-day fare lets you get on and off.

Known internationally for its optical sciences department, the *University of Arizona* (520–621–5130; www.arizona.edu) also has a number of other outstanding programs, including its basketball team, which has made it to the NCAA Final Four three times and, in 1997, won the NCAA championship! The school has produced such NBA stars as Sean Elliott, Brian Williams, and Steve Kerr. The older part of the campus, just through the main gate on University Boulevard, contains a number of interesting buildings and museums. Among them are *Centennial Hall,* which is a performing arts venue, *Old Main,* which is the school's first classroom, and the *Center for Creative Photography,* which holds an archive of photographs from Ansel Adams and Alfred Steiglitz and features rotating and traveling exhibits.

The University of Arizona Museum of Art (520–621–7567; art museum.az.edu) at 1031 North Olive on the University of Arizona campus has an impressive collection that ranges from pre-Renaissance to twentieth century, including works by Dürer, Rembrandt, Matisse,

Picasso, O'Keefe, and Audubon. The museum is open weekdays 9:00 A.M.–5:00 P.M. and Sunday noon–4:00 P.M. Closed on holidays. The *Arizona State Museum* (520–621–6302) is also part of the university. It specializes in American Indian cultures of the Southwest and northern Mexico and is recognized as one of the world's finest resources for artifacts (100,000 plus). More than 25,000 ethnographic objects also make up the collection. The museum is open weekdays 8:00 A.M.–5:00 P.M. Closed on holidays.

Just west of campus is the *Arizona Historical Society* (520–628–5774) at 949 East Second Street. Permanent and rotating exhibits display the state's past, and user-friendly archives are available for those who want to look up any arcane lore about Tucson. The historical society also holds annual events such as La Fiesta de San Agustin, a two-day celebration of Tucson's patron saint. The fiesta, held in fall, features Mexican and Native American music and entertainment, games for adults and kids, and food.

East of campus is the *Arizona Inn* (800–933–1093), which is on the National Register of Historic Places, across Campbell Avenue at 2200 East Elm. This 1930 hacienda-style hotel not only exudes charm but has the dual advantages of being near the center of town yet isolated enough to provide peace and quiet to its guests. It's a good place to visit in spring and fall just to stroll through the flower-bedecked inner courtyard. The inn is a popular spot for weddings and formal dinners. Visiting celebrities who want to eschew the big resorts often bunk here.

If you seek not celebrities but celebrated food with a Spanish accent, take a quick trip to *South Tucson,* a separate 1-square-mile city within Tucson's borders. Head south on Tucson Avenue until you can exit onto 22nd Street, then go west on 22nd until you reach South 4th Avenue and head south.

There are several Mexican restaurants and cafes in this area, including *Guillermo's Double L Restaurant* (520–792–1585) at 1830 South 4th Avenue. This establishment features Sonoran cuisine, a hybrid created by the indigenous peoples of Northern Mexico using Native American and Spanish influences. If you're bored with bland, fast-food-style tacos, enchiladas, and the like, you'll be pleasantly surprised at the variety of flavors Sonoran cuisine employs. One caveat for diners: Expect crowds on weekends. Hosts or hostesses may tell you there is a twenty-minute wait—it may actually be closer to forty minutes. You can spend your wait watching the colorful low-riding cruisers out on the boulevard.

The east side of Tucson has its own **Saguaro National Park East** (520–733–5153). To reach Saguaro National Park, take Broadway east to Old Spanish Trail and follow the signs. It doesn't offer the dramatic sunset views of Saguaro National Park West, but it's nearly 50,000 acres larger than the west side park. Stop at the Saguaro National Park East visitors center (open 8:30 A.M.–5:00 P.M. daily) and ask about the condition and difficulty of the trails before doing any hiking here. There are some easy loop trails, but others are quite difficult. Rest rooms and picnic areas are available at both the east side and west side parks. During times of drought when the desert brush is especially dry, you may be asked not to use the barbecue grills.

The east side also has a wonderful, hidden arboreal getaway called **Sabino Canyon** (520–749–8700). Drive east on Tanque Verde Road to Sabino Canyon Road, go north and keep driving, and you'll wind up in the parking lot. Sabino Canyon has roadrunners that are so tame they eat out of your hand and tram rides that can take you through the canyon (no other vehicles are allowed). The tram also runs in the moonlight on certain days of the year. Experienced hikers who visit Sabino Canyon often choose to make the trek to Seven Falls—occasionally quite a spectacular swimming hole, depending on the rain. It's only about a 5-mile hike, but the ground can be quite rocky and the underbrush treacherous. A quicker way to get there is to ride the tram to the start of Bear Canyon Trail and then hike the last 2 miles.

Incidentally, Tanque Verde Road could probably win an award as one of the strangest-looking streets in Arizona. It has a variety of weird statuary along its route: a life-size Tyrannosaurus rex at the Kolb intersection, an ersatz castle at Golf 'n' Stuff, a sculpted metal fish jumping out of the dry Tanque Verde wash (river) onto the street, and a wagon sitting on top of boulders at Trail Dust Town (home to the **Dakota Cafe** at 6541 East Tanque Verde—a great place to get nouvelle cuisine with a Southwestern flair). Not far from the Tanque Verde strip is the **Tanque Verde Guest Ranch** (800–234–3833; www.torqueverderanch.com) at 14301 East Speedway. It's an authentic, Old West–style dude ranch that was even used as the location for the Nickelodeon series *Hey Dude*. It has stables, tennis courts, and gourmet dining. Accommodations here are surprisingly luxurious, and the foothills setting is incomparable.

If you packed some formal attire and a charge card with a healthy limit, you might want to try the Five-Diamond **Tack Room** (520–722–2800) at 7300 East Vactor Road. The Tack Room features continental cuisine and an extensive wine list. Just look for the huge boot that serves as its sign on Sabino Canyon Road.

Tucson's West Side

From south Tucson, backtrack to Speedway Boulevard and head west. Pretty soon you'll notice that the cacti begin to outnumber the houses. Speedway becomes Gates Pass Road, and suddenly you're in the heart of **Saguaro National Park West** (928–733–5153), a terrific place to watch sunsets and take pictures, especially in the spring when the saguaros burst into white blossoms. The park was created to preserve the majestic saguaro cactus, which only grows in the Sonoran Desert. It can take a saguaro ten years to reach an inch in height and fifty-plus years before it grows arms. It's not unusual for a saguaro to be more than one hundred years old, although they're frequently killed off by frost, fire, and bacterial infection. State laws protect these mighty cacti from damage or theft. Several hiking or biking trails run through the park. They range from easy to moderately difficult. Before you start off on any of them, stop by the visitors center and talk to a park ranger. If you've never hiked in the desert before, it presents its own set of challenges.

An interesting attraction on this side of the city is the **Arizona-Sonora Desert Museum** (520–883–2702) at 2021 North Kinney Road. It features only plants and animals native to this part of the world. You can see everything from mountain lions and Mexican wolves to bark scorpions. The museum also has an extensive mineral collection. During summer the museum often holds special evening events so that visitors can get a look at bats, night-blooming cacti, and other nocturnal phenomenon. Museum hours vary; call for information. Tucson is also brimming with entertaining options for experiencing the best of the Old West. **Old Tucson Studios** (520–883–0100), located just down the road from the Desert Museum, underwent an extensive $13-million reconstruction project made necessary by a devastating 1995 fire. Cowpokes and wanna-bes will find western-themed buildings, rides, and shows.

If casino gambling is your sort of amusement, you're in luck—and you're also adhering to a Tucson tradition. Wyatt Earp and Doc Holliday used to play faro here in the 1880s. Take Valencia Road west, and turn south onto Camino de Oeste. You're now on the **San Xavier** (depending upon your facility with Spanish, you can try to pronounce the first syllable or simply say "Hah-veer") **Indian Reservation.** This is Pascua Yaqui land, and the tribe operates the **Casino of the Sun** (800–344–9435) at 7406 South Camino de Oeste, an enterprise that includes 500 gaming machines, high stakes bingo, and live keno, poker, and blackjack. And if you're hungry, the casino offers an all-you-can-eat prime rib buffet.

Saguaro National Park

The reservation also is the location of **Mission San Xavier del Bac** (520–294–2624) at 1950 West San Xavier Road. The fabled "White Dove of the Desert" is one part museum (containing artifacts and paintings that are several hundred years old) and one part Jesuit church, with regular services and many weddings. It's common to run into a wedding party while you're visiting the mission. You can take a self-guided tour of the church if there isn't a mass or other service going on. Also venture across the courtyard, and you'll find shops selling Native American crafts and vendors offering frybread and other goodies.

On the east side of the reservation, on land deeded to the Tohono O'Odham Indians, sits the **Desert Diamond Casino** at 7350 Old Nogales Highway. It has nearly everything the Casino of the Sun has except the live card games. Both casinos have slots with progressive jackpots and opportunities to win vehicles. Both have fast-food eateries.

Closer to town, off Oracle and Ina Roads, is **Tohono Chul Park** (520–575–8468) at 7366 North Paseo del Norte. This preserved site of natural Sonoran Desert has an easy-to-follow trail through forty acres that contain about 400 varieties of native plants. Wrens, quails, roadrunners, and other birds frequent the park, and you may see a cottontail rabbit or two. Year-round the park hosts demonstrations on low-water landscaping, lectures on Southwestern history, and seasonal events. Tohono Chul also has an art gallery that shows Southwestern artists and a tearoom in a hacienda-style home with a plant-filled courtyard. The park is open from 7:00 A.M. to sunset, with occasional after-hours events.

Santa Cruz County

Mexico is only about an hour's drive south from Tucson, and to get there you pass through the tail end of Pima County into *Santa Cruz County* (928–284–3685), an area with an oxcart load of history and rustic charm. The state's name actually originated in this region, where the Tohono O'Odham Indians called the land Arizonac, meaning "place of little springs."

Take the Nogales Highway off-ramp from I–10, and you'll merge onto I–19. For part of the next 20-mile stretch—where signs begin to show both miles and kilometers—there isn't much to see out the window: shrubs, sand, and an occasional patch of intense greenness where palo verde and mesquite have taken root. The scenery, however, zips by quite quickly, delivering motorists to the town of *Green Valley* (520–625–7575; www.greenvalleyazchamber.com). As the name implies, Green Valley is as verdant as a garden show. Set into a valley created by the Santa Rita Mountains, this Pima County community of about 20,000 was started some three decades ago as a retirement haven. The close-knit nature of Green Valley is in evidence everywhere. You won't find graffiti, litter, or abandoned buildings. The streets are clean, and the people are friendly. Lots of shops for groceries, restaurants—such as *Manuel Mexican Restaurant* (520–648–6068) at 75 West Calle de Las Tiendas and the long-established *Arizona Family Restaurant* (520–625–3680) at 80 West Esperanza—and a half-dozen golf courses make the town appealing to vacationers.

Just north of Green Valley is also the site for the *Titan Missile Museum* (520–625–7736), a National Historic Landmark on DuVal Mine Road. In the early 1980s, when the Titan II missile silos were deactivated, all but this one were destroyed. Green Valley's silo is the same today (minus the warhead, of course) as it was when it was part of America's defense program. Guided tours are available of the control room, the crew living quarters, and the missile launch area. The museum contains aircraft and mockups of early space capsules. Tours cost $7.50, and begin at 9:00 A.M.; the last one leaves at 4:00 P.M.

About 10 miles south on I–19 is Santa Cruz County and the tiny town of *Amado,* a ranching community with a few shops and restaurants. The best-known restaurant is the *Cow Palace* (520–398–2201) at 28802 South Nogales Road. It's a chuckwagon-cuisine kind of place with decor that includes framed photos of Western movie stars who have dined there.

Another five minutes or so away on I–19 is *Tubac,* the oldest city in the state—established in 1752 as a Spanish settlement and, today, sort of Arizona's answer to the artists' colony of Santa Fe, New Mexico. The attractions in this community are close together, and walking or bicycling is the best way to get around. Park your car in one of the lots just off I–19, and stroll down Tubac's narrow streets. Shops and art galleries like *Maggie's in Tubac* (520–398–2007) and *Red Willow Indian Arts* (520–398–2154), both on Tubac Road, offer handcrafted jewelry and crafts items. The community has a yearly arts festival in winter and a fall historic reenactment of the trek of Juan Bautista de Anza, the Spanish officer who passed through the area before he founded what would later become San Francisco. Be sure to see the *Tubac Presidio State Historic Park* (520–398–2252; www.pr.state.az.us) on Presidio Drive on the east side of town. The crumbling adobe remains of the original presidio wall (before the fort was relocated to Tucson) are here, along with an 1885 schoolhouse and a museum with exhibits detailing Spain's influence in this area. Also stop by *St. Ann's Church,* built in 1920 by a Bavarian carpenter.

When hunger pangs strike check out *Cafe Fiesta* (520–398–2332) at 19 Tubac Road. It serves salads, soups, and sandwiches.

Heading south on I–19 takes you to another historic spot: *Tumacacori National Historic Park* (520–398–2341), a collection of three Spanish colonial missions, including the *Tumacacori Mission.* Many visitors stop off just to photograph the mission, built by Franciscan friars and Native Americans in the early 1800s. Standing inside the weathered adobe rooms, you can see that the people who built this mission, which was an integral part of life in the Santa Cruz Valley during the 1800s, put a tremendous effort into the construction.

The best cultural experience of this trip may be 15 miles down the road in the city of *Nogales*. Nogales (the word means "walnut") is a town with a split personality. On the American side of the border, it seems like a sleepy bedroom community tucked into rolling hillsides. Here and there are spots of industry or commerce, especially along Grand Avenue, the city's main drag. The town has had more than its share of problems in recent years: political squabbles, pollution problems, and an economy that's especially dependent on the Mexican peso. Yet Nogales keeps plugging along, partly because many of the residents have family, friends, and business partners on the other side of the border. Additionally, 75 percent of all the winter fruits and vegetables consumed in the United States pass through this border.

It's what's south of the border that some visitors come to see. This is one of the few places where you can cross over into another country without a visa, passport, birth certificate, or any other identification. Be advised, however, that if you want to go farther south into Mexico, you will need some documentation, and you may have to put up a bond to take a vehicle or boat into the country. Call the *Immigration and Naturalization Service* at (520–670–4624) for complete details. The situation changes from time to time. You should also be aware that American auto insurance is not honored in Mexico. You should purchase relatively inexpensive Mexican insurance if you are taking your car across the border. There are a number of clearly marked insurance agencies on the American side where you can buy the necessary policy before taking your vehicle into Mexico. You may also consider parking your vehicle on the American side (you may have to pay a few dollars for a space) and walking across the border.

Nogales, in the Mexican state of Sonora, is definitely another world. The streets are narrow, and often the paving bricks are cracked or uneven. Much of the city isn't accessible to people in wheelchairs. Throughout the city you'll see many vendors clustered together under one awning. Everything is for sale here: jewelry, blankets, leather goods, electronics, arts and crafts, and liquor—especially the ever-popular Mexican specialties like tequila (made from the root of the agave cactus), kahlua (coffee liqueur), and cerveza (beer to you gringos and gringas). Luxury items like Cartier watches also are available here at duty-free rates. You can fill prescriptions here quickly and cheaply, and many Arizonans drive to Nogales to stock up on allergy medications and other drugs that are significantly pricier in the States. American currency is readily accepted and is often preferred over pesos.

Some of the products for sale are illegal in the States. Fireworks, switchblades (most made in Germany or Italy), and illegal drugs are among the most notable contraband. Mexican customs officials are usually pretty casual about waving people through at the border, but they will detain and search you if they think your behavior is suspicious. If you get into trouble on the Mexican side, don't expect the American guards to help you. Buyer (smuggler) beware!

Although you'll find a lot of friendly people (and some great bargains on glassware and silver jewelry if you're willing to haggle a little), you should be aware that shopkeepers eschew subtle sales tactics for the direct approach. They can be a bit forward at times, and some of the merchants think nothing of touching female customers in a manner considered inappropriate in the United States. There is also a dark side to Nogales. In recent years the problem of street kids mugging tourists has reared its ugly head. To play it safe, stay on well-traveled avenues and don't display any signs of wealth such as flashy jewelry, rolls of bills, expensive clothes, and camcorders. Keep away from the kids who approach you offering to do favors. Recently Nogales began using bilingual students to provide guidance to tourists, and the city has also beefed up police patrols in an effort to keep muggers away from the border area.

As for dining south of the border, it's wise to follow the standard rules for *touristas:* Don't drink the water unless it's in a restaurant advertising purified water, don't eat anything that's been undercooked, and don't purchase food from street vendors. You'll find Sonoran cuisine a little different from the Americanized version of Mexican food. Cheese is often goat cheese; the chili peppers tend to be hotter (even the innocent-looking habanéro, also known as "the gringo killer"); and a lot of seafood entrees are flavored with fresh lime juice. Prices at the better Nogales restaurants are about the same as in Arizona.

Did you know that Arizona has a *wine country?* Actually the history of grape growing in southeastern Arizona dates back to the conquistadores. After you've visited south of the border, you may want to explore a different side of the Grand Canyon State. Instead of taking I–19 back toward Tucson, take the freeway entrance to Route 82 east. You'll head north toward the town of *Patagonia* (520–394–0060). For nature lovers, this area is in itself a delight. The Nature Conservancy's *Patagonia-Sonoita Creek Preserve* (520–394–2400) is a cottonwood-willow riparian forest with trees as old as 130 years and as tall as 100 feet. More than 260 species of birds call the preserve home, including the gray hawk, green kingfisher, and violet-crowned hummingbird. There are also white-tail deer, javelina, and coyote. Many species of fish inhabit a perennial stream that runs through the preserve. Guided tours can be arranged through the Nature Conservancy.

Continuing north on Route 82, you'll find that while the state doesn't yet have the number of wineries and vineyards you'll find in California's wine country, the former ranch lands of *Sonoita* and *Elgin* are doing quite nicely in their current incarnations as grapefields. The vineyards that dot the hillsides of this gently rolling terrain include Callaghan, Arizona, Sonora, and Village of Elgin. Among the wineries, Callaghan is known for its Buena Suerte Cuvees. Many different varieties of table wine grapes are grown here. Approximately 20,000 cases of wine are produced annually by the winemakers in this region.

Depending on the time of year you visit, you may be able to watch a crush (usually in August), where you can see the grapes being stomped. April is the month for the Annual Wine Festival, when the fields are blessed by a coalition of clergy members. Whatever the month, you can drop by the **Chapel of Santa Maria,** an adobe territorial-style nondenominational shrine located in Elgin, just a tiny detour off Route 82.

This entire region was the site for many mines (copper, lead, silver, and gold), some of them in operation until the 1930s. Surrounding these mines were small communities, which sprang up in the 1850s to the 1880s. Now all long abandoned, these towns are little but crumbling adobe, not even worth the trouble to try to find. Many are on private property, so check with the Nogales/Santa Cruz Chamber of Commerce (520-287-3685) before wandering off. They can provide you with information on road conditions and which sites might still be worth visiting. One final word of caution if you do set off on your own: If you happen to come across a mine shaft, under no circumstances should you enter. Cave-ins are common; snakes and other creatures often take up residence in these locations; and caches of old, unstable dynamite have been found in shaft corridors.

Tombstone Area

J ust east of Santa Cruz County is **Cochise County,** once the stomping ground (and I mean that in the most literal sense) of Johnny Ringo, Wyatt Earp, and Doc Holliday. If your base of operations is Tucson, you can reach the historic towns of Benson, St. David, Tombstone, Sierra Vista, Bisbee, and Douglas by taking I–10 east until you reach Route 80, then heading south. You can also reach them from Santa Cruz County by taking Route 82 (which runs through Patagonia and Elgin) east to Route 80. Depending upon which direction you come from, you either arrive at Benson first (coming from Tucson) or Tombstone (from Sonoita).

For the sake of simplicity, let's assume you've driven down from Tucson.

Just before the Benson turnoff, you'll see a sign marked J–SIX RANCH ROAD/MESCAL. **Mescal,** to the north toward the mountains, is a dream factory. Since 1968 this make-believe town—a series of dirt streets and wooden buildings—has been the location for countless Western movies, TV shows, and commercials. Originally built for the Lee Marvin film *Monte Walsh,* it has since been used for the features *High Plains Drifter, Tom Horn, Tombstone,* and *The Quick and the Dead,* as well as the series *The Young Riders.* Unfortunately Mescal is strictly a closed set. Uninvited visitors are not allowed, and guards are posted to see to it that none show up. However, you can drive up the access road to the keep-out sign and with a good pair of binoculars you can easily make out many of the buildings.

Just down the road a bit is **Benson** (520–586–2842), situated in the San Pedro Valley. The scenery here is sporadically lush, with vistas that often include snowcapped mountains. A portion of the **San Pedro & South-western Railway** (520–586–2266) was recently restored, and weather permitting, you can take an open-air or enclosed, air-conditioned train ride on the *Frontier Flyer* from Benson to the ghost town of Fairbank. Passengers enjoy a scenic four-hour tour of the **San Pedro Riparian National Conservation Area** (520–458–3559). Western history buffs and bird-watchers find the leisurely trip fascinating as it meanders through the 40-mile-long valley where two thirds of North America's inland bird species have been spotted. Along the way, passengers learn about Cochise County's notorious Old West characters, including Doc Holliday, Geronimo, and Wyatt Earp. The railroad runs weekends October through May.

Bibliophiles may want to take a slight detour to the **Singing Wind Ranch Bookshop** (520–586–2425), north of I–10 via Ocotillo Road (turn at Singing Wind Road and look for the green gate with a chain). The bookshop's numerous offerings are grouped helter-skelter within a South-western ranch house, where hunting for buried treasures is as much fun as finding them. A treat for Benson's visitors is a stop at Lorene Whaley's **Horseshoe Cafe** (520–586–3303), 154 East Fourth Street. This two-story landmark has been in Whaley's family for decades, and, as a child, Wha-ley even lived upstairs in an apartment above the cafe. Burgers are mouthwatering, and the Mexican fare is good. The Horseshoe's giant cinnamon rolls are killer. It's a great spot for watching the trains go by and enjoying some down-home cooking.

Heading south on I–80 takes you through more riparian areas to the tucked-away town of **St. David.** Like much of southeastern Arizona, this peaceful little village was booming when nearby mines were open. Today you can enjoy browsing in antiques shops or visiting the **Holy Trinity Monastery** (520–720–4642). The monastery has a gift shop, library, meditation garden, museum, and other areas that are open to the public.

Tombstone (888–457–3929), "the town too tough to die," is only a few miles away from St. David on Highway 80. The story goes that the burg's founder (a prospector) was told that the only thing he would find in southern Arizona would be his tombstone—and the name stuck. The town had a much harder time sticking around than did the name. It was a prosperous mining community in the early 1880s, but by 1909 the community had fallen on hard times. It became prohibitively expensive to pull ore out of the nearby mines, which had flooded after miners had struck underground streams.

Driving into town, high on a hill to your left, you'll see the grave sites of infamous *Boot Hill* (520–457–9344), where the victims of the gunfight at OK Corral were buried. This wasn't, however, the original location for the cemetery; it was moved when the road was built. You can take a self-guided tour of the cemetery, photograph the sometimes comical markers (HERE LIES LESTER MOORE / FOUR SHOTS FROM A .44 / NO LES, NO MORE), and shop in the gift shop.

The community of Tombstone is rightfully proud of its place in American history. About $37 million in various ores was removed from the mines in its environs before they ceased operation. Even in the wild and woolly 1880s, the town of nearly 10,000 residents (now 1,500) had cultural activities, including literary societies, theater, and musical groups. Important mines-related events that occurred here were reported all over the country. Today Tombstone survives primarily because tourists who are fascinated with the Old West want to (as one sign puts it) WALK WHERE THEY [Western outlaws like the Clantons] FELL.

Allen Street in the heart of the historic section of Tombstone actually looks very much like a movie location, and this effect is heightened by staged gunfights that occur at regular times during *Helldorado Days* (usually October), *Nellie Cashman Rose Festival* (usually April), and other popular celebrations the town holds. Both sides of the boardwalk get crammed with camcorder-wielding tourists, as actors in 1880s attire shoot it out with black-powder firearms. Ironically the town has had a few problems with visitors brandishing real guns on the streets. So, as was the case in the days of Wyatt Earp, wearing firearms in town has been banned. Reenactors are exempt.

A number of souvenir shops line Allen Street, selling everything from T-shirts to Navajo jewelry.

On Allen and 6th Streets sits the *Bird Cage Theatre* (520–457–3421), a notorious gambling hall, saloon, and cathouse that operated from 1881 until 1889. The atmosphere was so wild in here that there are 140 bullet holes in the walls from gun battles. The Bird Cage Theatre is open daily for tours, and it's worth seeing as a good example of the type of place where frontier men entertained themselves. Hours are

8:00 A.M.–6:00 P.M. Theater tours cost $5.00 for adults, and there are discounts for children, seniors, and groups.

While you're on Allen Street, you may be tempted to pay the fee to walk around in the *OK Corral* (520–457–3456; www.ok-corral.com) at 308 Allen Street, Tombstone, AZ 85638. The live daily show is at 2:00 P.M. In all fairness it's worth a peek. You can tour exhibits of photographs of early Tombstone and read original newspaper accounts of the famous gunfight between the Clantons and the Earps. Inside the corral you can see life-size statues of the Earps and the Clantons arranged to represent the real participants of the shoot-out. The corral wasn't, however, the actual site of their armed altercation. The gunfight took place in 1881, in a vacant lot around the corner, across the street from where Fly's Boarding House once stood. The shooting lasted about a minute and occurred at nearly point-blank range. The final score: Morgan and Virgil Earp were seriously wounded; Doc Holliday was grazed by a round (he allegedly ran away in hysterics—a vicious killer, he was neither a good shot nor a brave man); Billy Clanton and Tom and Frank McLaury were shot dead. An excellent book on the subject is Paula Mitchell Marks's *And Die in the West,* which is available in bookstores on Allen Street.

On a happier note, Tombstone is also home to the *world's largest rose tree* (planted in the 1880s), located at the *Rose Tree Museum* (928–454–3326), just a short walk from Allen Street on Fourth and Toughnut. The rose tree is in the courtyard of a home that once belonged to Amelia Adamson, grown from a shoot given to her by the wife of a Scottish immigrant. The roses bloom from mid-March to mid-April, and even when the bush is dormant, you can enjoy the museum displays within the converted home. The displays recount life in early Tombstone. The museum is open daily 9:00 A.M.–5:00 P.M.

If hunger pangs get the better of you, try *Nellie Cashman's* (520–457–2212) at Fifth and Toughnut. Located in a historic building and named after one of the town's leading citizens of the 1880s, this traditional American restaurant has Western memorabilia on the walls and a menu that includes salads, sandwiches, steaks, chicken, hamburgers, and homemade pie. The *Longhorn Restaurant* (520–457–3405) at Fifth and Allen Street also offers American cuisine in addition to a little peek at history: Virgil Earp was shot and killed by a gunman firing from one of the Longhorn's second-story windows.

If you decide to stay in Tombstone, try *Priscilla's Bed & Breakfast* (520–457–3844) at Third and Safford. This B&B is a restored Victorian home that's been decorated in period splendor. Likewise, the *Tombstone*

Bordello Boarding House (520–457–2394) on Allen Street is an historic adobe home that reflects a time when the West was wilder. One of the town's newspapers is the *Tombstone Epitaph* (the other one is the *Tombstone Tumbleweed)*, considered Arizona's oldest newspaper. Featured prominently in TV series like *Wyatt Earp* and *Bat Masterson,* the more than one-hundred-year-old paper is published by the University of Arizona's journalism department.

Bisbee, Douglas, and Sierra Vista

Continuing south on Route 80 takes you to another historic place: *Bisbee* (520–432–5421; www.bisbeearizona.com) formerly a mining town, and now best known as an artists' community and a retreat for celebrities. It has recently been heralded by *Travel and Leisure* magazine as one of the "Best New American Destinations," comparing the century-old town with such world-renowned arts destinations as Aspen and Santa Fe. Set in the Mule Mountains, the older section of Bisbee (which can easily be covered on foot but is not particularly accessible for wheelchairs) may remind you a bit of San Francisco. The wooden Victorian buildings that dot the hillside and line the narrow main street have maintained their quaint charm. To find your way around, park in the first lot you come to as you enter town on Route 80, and walk across the street to the *Chamber of Commerce* office. They can give you maps of the area, as well as information on any events—poetry readings, music festivals, art openings—that may be taking place that day.

Next, you may want to wander into the *Bisbee Mining and Historical Museum* (520–432–7071) on Main Street (just look for the train out front). The museum details Bisbee's mining history and has displays of minerals that were found in and around the Mule Mountains. It also offers a glimpse into the town's past by describing its transition from boom to bust. The museum is open daily 10:00 A.M.–4:00 P.M.

While in the older section of Bisbee, you may want to take the underground tour of the *Queen Mine* (520–432–2071) on Arizona Street. The tour guides are former Queen Mine workers who take visitors deep into the defunct mine aboard original miniature train cars. Be sure to stop by the grand *Copper Queen Hotel* (520–432–2216; www.copper queen.com) on Howell Avenue, where Theodore Roosevelt once stayed and which continues to operate as a hotel and a restaurant. Rumor has it that a few friendly spirits inhabit the rooms of this classic hotel. For that matter, walking through the antiques shops lining Main Street is a trip back in time.

Antiques buffs and visitors looking for one-of-a-kind treasures will find Bisbee's winding streets a virtual paradise. Galleries, boutiques, gem shops, and antiques stores are plentiful, offering everything from locally mined Bisbee Blue turquoise to original art—much of it is created by local artisans.

Christina Plascencia's *55 Main Gallery* (520–432–4694) displays original art, clothing, and handcrafted jewelry. She even brings in psychics to entertain browsers in the gallery she describes as "a holistic venue for showing the essence of Bisbee . . . something for mind, body, and spirit." *Jane Hamilton Fine Art* (520–529–4886) showcases paintings, raku, and glass at 29 Main Street. *The Hunting Crow* (520–432–7757) serves up Native American art, jewelry, pottery, baskets, and gems. Overlooking the Lavendar Pit Mine, *Bisbee Blue Jewelry* (520–432–5511) sells its trademarked Bisbee Blue turquoise unusual shades of blue and green turquoise—set in silver.

Dining is equally eclectic in this historic hillside burg. *Cafe Roka* (520–432–5153) is gaining a well-deserved reputation for its gourmet fare presented in a historic storefront along the main drag. Another historic spot, the *Brewery Restaurant* (520–432–3317), fires up mesquite-grilled steaks and ribs, fresh seafood, and pasta seven days a week at 15 Brewery Gulch. Upstairs Bisbee's old stock exchange is the site for the *Stock Exchange Bar,* which attracts a diverse crowd and is prominently adorned with the original 1920s stock board that covers an entire wall.

Besides the aforementioned Copper Queen, there are several comfortable, unique places to stay in town. The *School House Inn* (800–537–4333) at 818 Tombstone Canyon is, as the name implies, a former school house. It has airy yet cozy rooms with private bathrooms. The *Oliver House* (520–432–4286) at 26 Soules is a bit of a hike from the main drag but has a lot of Victorian charm.

For nostalgia fanatics perhaps the only logical lodging choice would be the *Shady Dell Vintage Trailer and RV Park* (520–432–3567). This cluster of seven restored vintage Airstream trailers ranges from a 1935 "Niagara Honeymooner" to a 1957 "El Rey" and is located near the town's traffic circle. Each RV is furnished with period artifacts, chenille bedspreads, and radios tuned to swing music. Rates are from the past, as well, with accommodations available for less than $50. Adjacent to the Shady Dell is another period treasure, an actual refurbished diner that serves up the standard diner grub.

From Bisbee you can either continue along Route 80 to Douglas (520–364–2477), almost on the Mexican border, or you can backtrack north on Route 80 and take Route 90 west to Sierra Vista.

Let's consider **Douglas** first. One reason for making the drive to Douglas is to cross the border for a shopping trip in Agua Prieta (*ah-wah pree-etta*, meaning "dark water"); others are to romp in the surrounding Coronado National Forest or to visit the Gadsden Hotel.

Agua Prieta, a city of about 100,000, is headquarters to many *maquiladoras* (Mexican factories built by American companies) and features the same sort of Old World shopping you'll find in Nogales. If you're suffering from buyer's remorse because you passed up a *gonga* (bargain), you have a second shot at it.

On the north side of the border, the **Coronado National Forest** (520–670–4552) is an area ringed with mountain ranges, most notably the Dragoons to the northwest, the Peloncillo mountains to the east, and the Chiricahuas to the northeast. The Dragoons are the location of the fabled Cochise Stronghold, the last battle site for the legendary Native American leader. The Chiricahuas are known for being a bird-watcher's paradise, providing haven for varieties like the elegant trogon.

History buffs can take a detour on the Geronimo Trail to the restored **"Texas John" Slaughter Ranch** (520–558–2474), about 17 miles east of Douglas—and truly off the beaten path! Slaughter, a former Texas ranger, was the sheriff of Cochise County during the late 1880s. He is credited with running a lot of the riffraff out of the area. The Slaughter Ranch Museum is open Wednesday through Sunday.

If comfort and a certain early twentieth-century elegance are what you're looking for in lodgings, check into **The Gadsden Hotel** (520–364–4481; www.theriver.com) on G Avenue. The Gadsden was built in 1907 as a grand hotel for cattle barons and other well-heeled travelers, including Wilford Brimley, Paul Newman, Eleanor Roosevelt, Amelia Earhart, Johnny Depp, Faye Dunaway, Lee Marvin, and Jerry Lewis. Natasia Kinsski and Charlie Sheen called the Gadsden home during the filming of *Terminal Velocity*. It, too, is rumored to be inhabited by a few friendly ghosts! It boasts a lobby with an Italian marble staircase and four marble columns decorated in fourteen-karat gold leaf. This hotel, listed on the National Register of Historic Places, is a completely modern facility with air-conditioned rooms, apartments and executive suites with kitchenettes, and convention facilities.

Church Square on East E Avenue is believed to be the only place in the world with four churches on four corners in the same block. Once you've seen Douglas, you can either head west to Sierra Vista or north up to Willcox.

The city of *Sierra Vista* (520–452–0878 or 800–288–3861; www. vistasierravista.com) can be reached by taking I-10 east from Tucson to Route 90, or by taking Route 80 west to Route 90. Those who think of southeastern Arizona as vast stretches of vacant desert are in for a shock when they near Sierra Vista. The area around the town has not only the mountain views its name promises but also long expanses of palo verde, mesquite, and grasslands. A short distance from Sierra Vista are Garden Canyon and Ramsey Canyon Preserve. *Garden Canyon,* on the nearby Fort Huachuca property, is usually open for visitors and is a good place for bird-watchers to spot elegant trogons, Montezuma quail, and even northern pygmy owls. *Ramsey Canyon Preserve* (520–378–2785), which is protected by the Nature Conservancy, is a great place for hummingbird watching and just one of the many reasons Sierra Vista is known as the "Hummingbird Capital of the World." This proliferation of winged wonders (fourteen species) is the cornerstone of the annual Southwest Wings birding festival that takes place every August in Sierra Vista and surrounding habitats. It's even possible on occasion to take part in banding the tiny, colorful creatures. For more information about hummingbird banding, write to Ramsey Canyon Preserve, 27 Ramsey Canyon Road, Hereford, AZ 85615. At the preserve's entrance, the *Ramsey Canyon B&B* (520–378–3010) has modern accommodations and freshly baked pies. Space in these facilities books fast! Just outside the preserve is a new addition to the county, the nonprofit *Arizona Folklore Preserve.* There Arizona's Official Balladeer, Dolan Ellis, entertains visitors with the songs, legends, and poetry of the Old West, accompanied by stunning photographic images he has collected. The Arizona Folklore Preserve is open on weekends for performances by Ellis (a former member of the New Christy Minstrels) and other folk artists and is dedicated to the collection, presentation, and preservation of Arizona folklore.

Fort Huachuca (520–533–5736) is just a few minutes west of Sierra Vista. An Army base that today serves as headquarters for the U.S. Army's Intelligence Center and Information Systems Command, the fort's history stretches back to the 1870s, when it was established as a camp to protect settlers against Apache raiders. It has had an interesting history as a base

The San Pedro River in southeastern Arizona's Cochise County actually flows northward into the United States from Mexico.

for the soldiers who tracked down Geronimo and the troops who battled Pancho Villa, as well as home for the African-American cavalry units that came to be known as the "buffalo soldiers." The fort had its ups and downs after World War II. It even closed for a while. In 1954 it was turned into the Army's electronic proving ground. One former soldier who served at the fort in the 1950s is a well-known speaker on the UFO circuit. He claims that he saw the Army test extraterrestrial aircraft there, though no proof of his claims exists. A history museum is dedicated to the various incarnations of Fort Huachuca.

Modern accommodations and charming bed-and-breakfast inns are plentiful in Sierra Vista, with nearly 900 rooms available. The nicest full-service hotel is the 148-room *Windemere Hotel & Conference Center* (800–825–4656 or 520–459–5900; www.reservations@winde merehotel.com) at 2047 South Highway 92, located a few miles from the turnoff for Ramsey Canyon.

Northern Cochise County

ou can reach historic sites like the Chiricahua National Monument and the adobe ruins of *Fort Bowie* by taking Route 90 from Sierra Vista; take I–10 to Willcox, and then follow Route 186 to *Chiricahua National Monument* (520–824–3560). Here are many huge stone towers surrounded by pine and juniper forests. Take the Bonita Canyon Drive through the monument, and you'll reach the top of Massai Point. You can park here and get a terrific view of the Chiricahua Mountain range, known as the "Wonderland of Rocks." Picnic tables and rest rooms are available at marked areas within the monument. North of the monument is *Fort Bowie National Historic Site* (520–847–2500; ww.nps.gov/fobo/). It was established in 1862 to protect travelers from Apache raids. Today all that remains of the fort are crumbling adobe walls. A museum on the grounds displays exhibits illustrating the fort's history. An easy $1\frac{1}{2}$-mile walk from the fort is a trail used almost 140 years ago by Butterfield stagecoaches and a cemetery where the son of Apache leader Geronimo is buried.

If you take Highway 181 heading northwest, the next town you reach is *Willcox* (800–200–2272), located in the Sulphur Springs Valley, an agricultural paradise. More than two dozen farms grow everything from apples to chilis to pecans. Harvest seasons vary, but many range from late July through late September or early October. Some of these farms allow you to pick your own produce, and you can get a brochure with a list of the farms and a map from Willcox Chamber of Commerce, 1500 North Circle I Road, Willcox, AZ 85643. The chamber is also home to the *Chiricahua Regional Museum* (520–384–2272), which chronicles the area's rich history and agriculture-based economy. The museum is open Monday through Saturday 10:00 A.M.–4:00 P.M.

If you'd prefer to sample nature's bounty without risking throwing your back out, you may want to drop by the nearby *Stout's Cider Mill* (520–384–3696) at 1510 North Circle I Road. It can be reached by taking exit 340 from I–10. The mill offers apple cider, ice cream, a variety of condiments and snacks, and several very tempting types of apple pie, including one with no added sugar or artificial sweeteners. Stout's Cider Mill is open daily year-round.

West of Willcox just off I–10 resides the museum housing the infamous *Thing.* This "Thing" isn't the hand from the *Addams Family* series or the creature from either the John Carpenter or the Howard Hawks science fiction films. It's the *other* thing. The one advertised on the giant yellow billboards you can't help but see unless you drive through southeastern Arizona with your eyes closed. The "museum" (for want of a better description) housing "The Thing?? Mysteries of the Ages" is a barnlike building that for about three-and-a-half decades also has contained a variety of antiques. Its proud centerpiece is a mummylike figure encased in glass. No one knows for certain if this is a genuine mummy. (It's possible: Some cliff-dwelling Native American tribes, including the Anasazi, tucked their dead away in places out of reach of scavengers, and more than a few of these bodies have been recovered.) In any case, you can get in for less than a buck, and I recommend the museum to Stephen King aficionados, lovers of roadside Americana,

Cowboy Singer Rex Allen

*W*illcox's favorite son unquestionably is cowboy singer Rex Allen, whose film, television, and recording career is celebrated at the Rex Allen Arizona Cowboy Museum (520–384–4583) at 150 North Historic Railroad Avenue. The museum also contains exhibits about frontier settlers and the cowboy way of life. The museum is open daily 10:00 A.M.–4:00 P.M. Willcox hosts an annual Rex Allen Days festival the first weekend in October. Featured events include a rodeo, a parade, and stage shows.

and anyone who grew up in the 1950s or 1960s who read EC or Warren horror comics ("Look, Johnny—that thing is moving! EEYYYIII!").

Even if you're not wrapped up in mummies, you'll find that the scenery around Willcox is quite lovely. In places this high-desert community barely resembles the Southwest. Nowhere is this more apparent than on the marshlike *Willcox Playa Wildlife Refuge,* just south of town. Bird-watchers may want to plan a visit to occur between late October and mid-February to catch a glimpse of the sandhill cranes that nest in the playa. Sandhill cranes are believed to be one of the oldest species of birds. Standing four feet tall with a five-to-seven-feet wingspan, they are quite spectacular. Each January Willcox stages a major celebration of the cranes' arrival (by the thousands) during the *Wings over Willcox* event.

Also south of Willcox on Route 666 is *Cochise Stronghold* (520–826–3593). This national monument is the site where the legendary chief of the Chiricahua Apaches made his final stand against the U.S. Army. He is buried within the monument, though no one knows the exact location. The area, both rugged and serene, is home to a variety of wildlife and offers a number of picnic areas and campsites. Hiking trails are well marked but can be quite difficult because of the elevation and the rocky nature of the terrain.

PLACES TO STAY IN SOUTHERN ARIZONA

GREEN VALLEY
Viscount Suite Hotel,
4855 East Broadway,
85711;
(520) 745–6500.
Microwaves and refrigerators in all suites; three restaurants.

PEARCE
Grapevine Canyon Ranch,
P.O. Box 302, 85625;
(520) 826–3185 or
(800) 245–9202;
fax: (520) 826–3636;
www.gcranch.com.
Open year-round. Eleven rooms nestled in a picturesque canyon in rugged Dragoon Mountains 80 miles southeast of Tucson.

TUCSON
Westin La Paloma,
3800 East Sunrise Drive,
85718;
(520) 742–6000 or
(800) 677–6338.
487 rooms, spa, water slide, five restaurants, stunning views.

Arizona Inn,
2200 East Elm Street,
85719;
(520) 325–1541,
(800) 933–1093;
fax: (520) 881–5830.
Centrally located, historic, charming, extensive gardens.

Hampton Inn Tucson,
1375 West Grant Road,
85745;
(520) 206–0602.
All rooms have microwaves and refrigerators, breakfast bar, heated pool.

The Hilton Tucson East,
7600 East Broadway Boulevard, 85710;
(520) 721–5600.
Full-service atrium hotel with spacious rooms offering mountain views.

YUMA
Radisson Suites Inn Yuma,
2600 South Fourth Avenue,
85364;
Hotel-motel with pool and spa pool, plus laundry.

PLACES TO EAT IN SOUTHERN ARIZONA

TOMBSTONE
Longhorn Restaurant,
5th Street and Allen (across from Crystal Palace),
85638;
(520) 457-3405.
For good steaks in Old West ambience.

Don Teodoro's,
15 North Fourth Street,
85638;
(520) 457-3647.
Authentic Mexican fare in a funky atmosphere.

TUCSON
El Charro Mexican Cafe & Gift Shop,
311 North Court Avenue,
85701;
(520) 622-1922;
fax: (520) 628-4188.
Oldest family-operated Mexican restaurant in the United States, with a long tradition of spicing things up!

Luby's Cafeteria,
7140 East Rosewood,
85710;
(520) 290-9086.
Lots of choices, moderately priced, everything prepared fresh on-site every day including fresh baked breads.

Sweet Tomatoes,
6202 East Broadway Boulevard, 85711;
(520) 747-4137;
or 4420 North Stone Avenue;
(520) 293-3343.
All you care to eat from a buffet of fresh salads, from-scratch soups, and hot muffins.

YUMA
Martinez Lake Restaurant and Cantina,
West end of Martinez Lake Road, 85365;
(928) 783-0253.
Overlooking the water with a full menu and live music twice a week. Worth the thirty-minute drive from downtown Yuma.

Web Sites for Southern Arizona

Cochise County:
www.arizonaguide.com/cochise

Metropolitan Tucson Convention & Visitors Bureau:
www.arizonaguide.com/visittucson

Sierra Vista:
www.arizonaguide.com/sierravista

General Attractions Index

Entries for museums, accommodations, and restaurants appear in the special indexes on pages 162-166.

INDEXES

Tombstone, 143
Tonto National Forest, 112
Tonto Natural Bridge State Park, 80
Toroweap Point, 3
Tortilla Flat, Arizona, 112
Train Depot, 127
Truxton, 42
Tseghahodzani, 66
Tubac, 139
Tubac Presidio State
    Historic Park, 139
Tucson, 128
Tucson Arts District, 130
Tumacacori Mission, 139
Tumacacori National Historic
    Park, 139
Turf Soaring School, 87
Turquoise Ladies, 81
Tuzigoot National Monument, 50

U
Unicorn Balloon Company, 87
University of Arizona, 133
Upton House, 107

V
Valentine, 42
Valley of the Sun, 85
Verde Canyon Railroad, 50
Verkamp's Curio, 21
Vermillion Cliffs, 5
Vulcans Throne, 20
Vultee Arch, 25
Vulture Mine, 106

W
Wahweap Lodge and Marina, 8
Walnut Canyon National
    Monument, 16
Watchtower, 20
Western States Motorcycle Tours, 85
Whiskers, 52
Whiskey Row, 55
White House Ruins, 67
White Mountains Apache
    Reservation, 76
Wickenburg, 106
Wilderness River Adventures, 9
Willcox, 150
Willcox Playa Wildlife Refuge, 152
Williams, 17
Window Rock, 65
wine country, 141
Wings over Willcox, 152
Winslow, 72
Winslow Municipal Airport, 73
Winterfest, 13
World Jet-Ski Racing Finals, 48
world's largest rose tree, 145
World's Oldest Rodeo, The, 79
Wupatki National Monument, 10

Y
Yuma, 119
Yuma Crossing State Historic
    Park, 119
Yuma River Tours, 124
Yuma Territorial Prison State Park,
    The, 121
Yuma Valley Railroad, 124

Museums and Sights

Bed-and-Breakfast Inns, Inns, Lodges, Motels, and Guest Ranches

Restaurants, Cafes, and Other Eateries

About the Author

Tucson-based journalist Scott Barker has lived in Arizona for almost forty years and has traveled extensively throughout the state. He is the recipient of awards from the Arizona Author's Association and the Arizona Press Club.

About the Editor

Jill Bean Florio is a travel writer living in Flagstaff, Arizona. A former wilderness guide with Voyageur Outward Bound, she loves to hike, bike, paddle, run, cave, and climb throughout the West. Jill is the arts editor for *Flagstaff Live;* writes for *Sweat Magazine, Trail Runner, Mountain Living Magazine,* and *Travelwise;* and manages the sports and recreation community at www.suite101.com. She is currently working on climbing, caving, and other outdoor travel guides for Globe Pequot Press.